The Braun Hand Blender Cookbook

The Braun Hand Blender Cookbook

By Joie Warner

A Penguin/Flavor Publications Book

First published 1988 by
Penguin Books Canada Limited
2801 John Street
Markham, Ontario L3R 1B4

CANADIAN CATALOGUING IN PUBLICATION DATA
Warner, Joie
    The Braun hand blender cookbook
Includes index.
ISBN 0-14-046851-X
1. Blenders (Cookery).   I. Title.
TX840.B5W37 1988   641.5'89   C88-094746-2

This book was designed, photographed, and produced by
Flavor Publications
278 Bloor Street East, Suite 408
Toronto, Ontario M4W 3M4

Cover photo: Cheddar Cheese Soup (page 132),
          Strawberry Cheesecake (page 180), and,
          Herbed Chicken Liver Pâté (page 22).

Printed and bound in Canada

ACKNOWLEDGEMENTS

I would like to thank Kristina Goodwin and Ruth Phelan for their invaluable help in the kitchen developing and testing recipes.

CONTENTS

SWEET AND SAVORY SAUCES AND DRESSINGS · 57

OMELETS AND EGG DISHES · 89

VEGETABLES - 161

DESSERTS - 179

INTRODUCTION

Until I was asked to develop and write recipes for this book, I thought I had every kitchen appliance I would ever need. Then I was introduced to the Braun hand blender — a utensil that blends, purées, and liquefies foods very fast and effortlessly. While there are blenders that blend and food processors that purée, the hand blender is truly a unique kitchen machine that does both, but much more conveniently. No wonder it has become a best-selling kitchen appliance.

Within moments of taking the blender out of its package, I was in the kitchen making mayonnaise. I was amazed at how easily and swiftly the hand blender emulsified the ingredients. If you have ever tackled making your own mayonnaise — or resisted because you thought it was too difficult — then you are in for a treat! There is no need to drizzle the oil in a fine stream (very hard on the wrist!) as you must do while hand whisking or whirling the ingredients in a food processor. With the hand blender all you need do is place the oil, eggs, and seasonings in the beaker together; place the hand blender in the beaker, turn it on for a few seconds and instantly you have wonderful, thick mayonnaise. Then with just a quick rinse under running water, the hand blender is clean and ready for its next task.

As I continued to test sauces such as hollandaise, béarnaise, salad dressings, and sweet sauces, I knew I had discovered the perfect tool for sauce-making. Moving on to soups, again I found the hand blender indispensable. The ability to take the hand blender to the saucepan — instead of having to pour the soup into the conventional blender container and back into the pan again — means quick and easy mixing and puréeing of ingredients right there, where you are preparing the food.

But the hand blender does more than emulsify and purée sauces, salad dressings, and soups in seconds. It works wonders with dips and spreads by combining and puréeing the ingredients, while at the same time allowing you to leave some interesting texture in the finished dish. The hand blender's unique design provides direct control of the blending process: it lets you process the ingredients from chunky to velvety smooth and anywhere in between.

The hand blender also whips up tasty compound butters to spread on muffins, breads, and vegetables; it whisks eggs into puffy omelets, frittatas, and soufflés; it turns out ethereal crêpes, pancakes, waffles, and batters; it purées vegetables and baby food; it makes frothy drinks and milkshakes and creates delectable desserts such as mousses, frostings, and pie fillings.

This book contains recipes for all of these things.

I have enjoyed creating these recipes specifically for the hand blender. They are an eclectic collection, and intentionally so, for I have included the homey and old-fashioned along with more innovative recipes to show the hand blender's versatility and proficiency.

Follow the recipes because they've all been tested and proven — and they taste good! But then, don't be afraid to substitute different herbs and spices, to change the thickness of soups and sauces by using light cream instead of heavy, to add more liquid to very thick milkshakes, or to change the textures of dishes by blending more or less than I have suggested. Be creative and make these recipes *your* recipes, especially by substituting and adapting them to what is freshest at the market.

I hope you'll enjoy making these dishes as much as I have and, even more important, that you'll also be inspired to use the Braun hand blender with many of your own favorite recipes.

Joie Warner

THE HAND BLENDER

The Braun hand blender was designed for those who believe the joy of cooking comes from creating — not from cleaning up. It performs the functions you'd normally ask of your conventional blender, but with greater ease, speed, and convenience.

As interest in food and cooking techniques has grown over the past 15 years, so has the range of kitchen appliances available to the home chef. The food processor has been a major addition to kitchens, saving cooks valuable time by facilitating the chopping and slicing processes.

But one old standby, the blender, had not been improved upon for years — until we created the Braun hand blender. We saw how so many old-style blenders had gone the route from kitchen counter to cupboard under the sink or to the garbage or storage locker. Why? Mainly because of the nuisance of transferring food back and forth into the old-style blender container, then cleaning up afterward. What was needed, we decided, was a truly portable blender. And so we set about developing one.

With the Braun hand blender, you take the blender to the food, not the food to the blender. You can complete a recipe in just one bowl or pot without any messy pouring back and forth. And when you've finished, the hand blender can be quickly cleaned with just a rinse under the tap.

Because it's so easy to use, the hand blender makes it a breeze to prepare dips, sauces, soups, milkshakes, and drinks that would otherwise be tedious. You need only use the Braun hand blender once to prepare mayonnaise to witness real magic in your kitchen. Then try it for everything from pancake batters to reconstituting frozen orange juice! Use it also to blend or smooth out lumps in gravy or canned soups.

We know you'll agree that the results are impressive.

There are presently two sizes of hand blender to choose from: *the MR300 series* and *the MR7 series.* These models vary in power, size, features — as shown in the chart opposite — and in price. And now, in addition to the hand blenders themselves, the new CA1 chopper attachment is available. It fits all models presently in the stores.

All Braun hand blenders feature the convenient wall mount attachment. This bracket keeps your blender ready to hand but also up and out of the way. All of our hand blenders also feature a beaker for mixing small quantities of food — ingredients to add to sauces, for example. But usually, you'll simply take your hand blender to the container that you're using to prepare or cook a given recipe.

The MR7 series features a variable speed control which allows you to use a whisk attachment (included with these models) for whipping egg whites, cream, or other light batters. Additional accessories on the deluxe models include a spatula, work bowl, and egg white separator.

The CA1 chopper attachment works as a really handy mini food processor. It can process up to 7 ounces (200-g) of meat, onions, parsley, cheese, and the like, which is 80 percent of what most other mini food processors can do. Best of all, the blade and bowl are dishwasher-safe, making them a snap to clean.

MODEL	POWER	FEATURES	OPTIONS
MR300	*100W*	• *Wall mount* • *Clear beaker with lid*	• *Fits CA1 chopper* *attachment*
MR72	*150W*	• *Wall mount* • *Variable speed* • *Whisk attachment* • *Beaker*	• *Fits CA1*
MR7	*150W*	• *Wall mount* • *Variable speed* • *Whisk attachment* • *Mixing bowl* • *Egg separator* • *Beaker*	• *Fits CA1*
CA1 Chopper		• *200g (7 oz.) capacity* • *Powered by the hand blender motor*	

Our Braun hand blender works in much the same way as a jug-style blender: by chopping or emulsifying food with rapidly moving blades. Like a jug blender, a hand blender works best on food with a more liquid or watery base. The rapidly moving blades pull the food up toward them and push the puréed food out the slots on the end. As you use the hand blender, you'll see the sauces or batters flow in this way.

If you're puréeing a heavier batter or solid food such as baby food or mashed potatoes, you'll have to push the blender through the food to ensure an evenly blended consistency. With more liquid batters, the hand blender will do most of the work for you and you can simply stir it around slowly to ensure the even consistency you require.

The Braun hand blender's greatest strengths are in puréeing and emulsifying food. It does both amazingly well. Do remember, though, that it can't handle a heavy batter like that for cakes or muffins or *aerate* foods without the whisk attachment that is available on the MR7 series models. This whisk whips air into egg whites, cream, and very runny batters.

But also keep in mind that the basic hand blender unit is not designed to chop dry foods like nuts or breadcrumbs. This is where the CA1 chopper attachment comes in. It will handle all of these chopping tasks with ease.

SOME USEFUL TIPS.

Once you understand how the Braun hand blender works, just follow these easy tips to make sure it does its very best for you.

1. Cut most solid food into ½-inch (1-cm) cubes for easy blending.
2. Be sure there are no fruit stones, bones, or other hard materials in the blending mixture as these will damage the blades.

3. Don't fill containers too full. The level of the mixture will rise during blending and an excess will cause it to overflow.

4. Don't pull the hand blender out of the mixture or put it into the mixture while it is running. Have it in place before switching it on. This way, you'll avoid splashing — especially important when working with a *hot* mixture!

5. We recommend that you remove hot sauces/soups from the heat while blending. This will reduce the risk of the hand blender overheating and also the risk of splashing with very hot food.

6. The Braun hand blender performs its work in seconds, not minutes. To maintain food texture as you require it, avoid overblending. Work in short bursts and watch the food carefully.

7. The hand blender works best if it is run in short bursts and never longer than 1 minute at any one time without interruption. If run for a full minute, it should then be allowed to rest for about 3 minutes. Running the blender for too long at a time may damage the motor.

8. Make sure you unplug the unit before cleaning. Then rinse the *blade part only* under running water.

9. For best results, clean the hand blender immediately after use. This is particularly important with foods that may stain, such as tomatoes, carrots, or beets.

10. If you own a hand blender without the variable speed the recipes will work just as well. Disregard the speed settings and use your own judgement.

IMPORTANT SAFEGUARDS.

When using electrical appliances, always follow these basic safety precautions:

1. Read all instructions first.

2. To protect against electrical hazards, do not immerse motor housing (base) in water or other liquid.

3. Supervise closely when any appliance is used by or near children.

4. Unplug appliance from outlet when not in use, before putting on or removing attachments, and before cleaning.

5. Do not operate any appliance with a damaged cord or plug, or if the appliance malfunctions, or has been dropped or damaged in any way. In such cases, return appliance to the nearest authorized service facility for examination, repair, or adjustment.

6. The use of attachments not recommended by the appliance manufacturer may cause hazards.

7. Do not use outdoors.

8. Do not let cord hang over edge of table.

9. Do not place on or near a hot gas or electrical burner, or in a heated oven.

10. Do not use appliance for other than intended use.

11. The hand blender operates on 110v/60 cycle AC only.

CHAPTER ONE

APPETIZERS, DIPS, BUTTERS, AND SPREADS

HERBED CHICKEN LIVER PÂTÉ

SMOKED SALMON PÂTÉ

PINE NUT BUTTER

HONEY PISTACHIO BUTTER

RED WINE AND APRICOT BUTTER

BRIE BUTTER

SHRIMP BUTTER

STILTON BUTTER

ASIAGO BUTTER

CROSTINI BUTTER

GREEN CHILI BUTTER

APPLE BUTTER

ANCHOVY BUTTER

REALLY GREEN SNAIL BUTTER

CAPER BUTTER

GOAT CHEESE AND SUN-DRIED TOMATO SPREAD

CRAB MOUSSE

SMOKED TROUT MOUSSE

ASPARAGUS TOASTS

CHEESE DREAMS (CHEDDAR CHEESE SPREAD)

FRESH DILL DIP

CHICKPEA DIP

CREAMY CURRY DIP

ROASTED RED PEPPER DIP

GREEN CHILI DIP

CHUTNEY CURRY CREAM CHEESE DIP

FETA ANCHOVY DIP

HOT CRAB AND CHEESE DIP

SARDINE SPREAD

AVOCADO DIP

Herbed Chicken Liver Pâté

2 slices bacon, chopped	½ teaspoon freshly ground
½ cup butter	black pepper
1 cup chopped onion	½ teaspoon salt
(about 1 medium)	¼ teaspoon allspice
1 garlic clove, chopped	1 pound chicken livers,
1 Granny Smith apple,	membrane removed and
peeled, cored, and chopped	quartered
1 tablespoon fresh dill	2 tablespoons rye whiskey,
1 teaspoon dried marjoram	brandy, or cognac
1 teaspoon dried thyme	¼ cup heavy cream
1 bay leaf	Garnish:
½ teaspoon freshly	Chopped fresh parsley
grated nutmeg	

In large heavy skillet, fry bacon in butter for 3 minutes. Add onion, garlic, and apple and cook over medium-high heat, stirring, for about 4 minutes or until soft. Stir in dill, marjoram, thyme, bay leaf, nutmeg, pepper, salt, and allspice; cook 2 minutes. Add chicken livers, rye, and cream; cook for about 5 minutes, stirring constantly, or until livers are just pink inside. Remove bay leaf; discard. Pour pâté mixture into mixing bowl, blend on #6 speed for about 1 minute or until smooth. Chill several hours in crock or serving dish. Garnish with chopped fresh parsley. Makes about 2½ cups.

SMOKED SALMON PÂTÉ

10 ounces smoked salmon, finely chopped	2 tablespoons heavy cream
	2 teaspoons fresh lemon juice
2 tablespoons minced onion	½ teaspoon freshly ground
1 tablespoon prepared hot horseradish	white pepper
	Garnish:
1 cup (8 ounces) cream cheese, at room temperature	Fresh dill

In mixing bowl, blend salmon, onion, and horseradish on #6 speed until smooth. Add cream cheese, cream, lemon juice, and pepper; blend until combined and smooth. Garnish with dill. Makes about 2⅓ cups.

This creamy, smooth, coral-colored pâté with wonderful salmon flavor makes a very elegant starter. Pipe mousse onto canapé bases or into hollowed-out cherry tomatoes and garnish with sprig of dill. Spread on melba toast, crackers, or cucumber slices and top with salmon caviar and dill sprigs.

PINE NUT BUTTER

1 cup pine nuts	2 tablespoons freshly grated
Freshly ground black pepper	Parmesan cheese, or to taste
½ cup butter, at room	
temperature	

In medium non-stick skillet, toast pine nuts and pepper over medium heat, stirring constantly with wooden spoon until nuts are golden, about 5 minutes. Make sure pine nuts do not become dark brown. Remove from heat. Set aside and cool.

In mixing bowl, blend pine nuts, butter, and cheese on #6 speed until smooth and combined. Makes about 1¼ cups.

This smooth beige butter has an extremely nutty, cheesy flavor. Beautiful over green beans, broccoli, asparagus, Brussels sprouts, baked potato, or pasta. Spread on hot crusty rolls, or smother on roasted chicken, steaks, chops, or broiled fish. It's also very tasty spread on a salmon fillet, then wrapped in phyllo pastry, brushed with butter, and baked. Serve this dish with Fresh Dill Dip (see page 46).

HONEY PISTACHIO BUTTER

¾ cup butter, at room temperature	3 tablespoons liquid honey
½ cup shelled pistachios, finely chopped*	½ teaspoon ground cinnamon

In mixing bowl, blend butter on #6 speed until smooth. Add nuts, honey, and cinnamon; blend again until smooth and thoroughly combined. Makes about 1¼ cups.

A sweet awakener to Sunday brunch spread on scones, toast, hot cross buns, croissants, or English muffins. For an interesting specialty cake, add cream cheese or cream to this butter and use it to layer sponge cakes, hazelnut tortes, or the like.
*To chop pistachios, place shelled pistachios in between wax paper and use a rolling pin to crush.

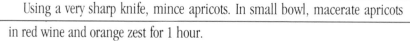

RED WINE AND APRICOT BUTTER

1 cup (8 ounces) dried apricots	3 tablespoons liquid honey
¼ cup dry red wine	¾ cup butter, at room temperature
Finely grated zest of 2 large oranges	

Using a very sharp knife, mince apricots. In small bowl, macerate apricots in red wine and orange zest for 1 hour.

In small saucepan, warm honey and add to apricots. In mixing bowl, place butter and blend on #6 speed until smooth. Stir in apricot mixture and blend until well combined. Makes about 2 cups.

It is important to mince the apricots finely or the texture will be too chunky. This makes a delicious spread on pancakes, waffles, crepes, French toast, and muffins. As it contains wine, this butter should not be frozen.

BRIE BUTTER

¼ cup butter, at room temperature	½ cup (4 ounces) Brie, rind removed, at room temperature and cubed

In mixing bowl, blend butter on #6 speed until smooth. Add Brie and blend until smooth and well combined. Makes about ¾ cup.

Rich and delicate in flavor, this butter can be spread on warm crusty brown bread, brioches, or French stick. Stuff chicken breasts or make a pocket in veal chops and stuff with this butter. It's also delicious on sandwiches, with noodles, or swirled into creamy soups. Great spread on canapé bases topped with pear slices or sliced meats. You can substitute Camembert for the Brie.

SHRIMP BUTTER

12 ounces shrimp, peeled and deveined	2 teaspoons fresh lemon juice
	¼ teaspoon Tabasco
½ cup butter, melted	¼ teaspoon salt
⅔ cup finely chopped onion	¼ teaspoon freshly ground
2 tomatoes, peeled, seeded, and chopped	black pepper

Using a very sharp knife, mince shrimp very finely — to a paste. Set aside.

In medium skillet, melt butter over medium heat. Add onion and tomato; cook for 15 minutes or until slightly thickened. Stir in shrimp paste, lemon juice, Tabasco, salt, and pepper. In skillet, blend on #6 speed until smooth. Transfer to a bowl and chill for several hours before serving. Makes about 2¼ cups.

Delicious spread on crackers, melba toast, or thinly sliced rye bread.

STILTON BUTTER

½ cup butter, at room temperature	12 ounces Stilton cheese, crumbled, and at room temperature

In mixing bowl, cream butter on #6 speed until smooth. Add Stilton gradually on #6 speed until well combined and smooth. Makes about 2 cups.

You can substitute any blue-veined cheese such as Gorgonzola, Danish blue, Cambozola, or Roquefort for the Stilton. A creamy butter with good bite, it's great spread on dark rye or slices of French bread and topped with seedless red or green grape halves. Try it on slices of French stick topped with lettuce, rare roast beef, horseradish, and sliced radishes. It's also delicious spread on apple or pear slices.

ASIAGO BUTTER

1½ cups (about 6 ounces) finely grated Asiago cheese	½ cup butter, at room temperature
1 cup (8 ounces) cream cheese, at room temperature	2 large garlic cloves, minced
	¼ teaspoon red pepper flakes

In mixing bowl, place Asiago, cream cheese, butter, garlic, and red pepper flakes and blend on #6 speed until smooth. Makes about 2¼ cups.

This butter has a wonderful, cheesy, sharp flavor. For a somewhat zestier tang, Parmesan or Romano cheese may be substituted for the Asiago. Serve with bread sticks or toss with pasta. Why not spread on an Italian bun and top with a hot Italian sausage and peperonata or your favorite relish?

CROSTINI BUTTER

1 cup butter, at room temperature	1 can (1.75-ounce/50-g) anchovy fillets, drained and chopped
3 large shallots, minced	
5 large garlic cloves, minced	1 teaspoon fresh lemon juice
2 tablespoons dried basil or ¼ cup chopped fresh	½ teaspoon freshly ground black pepper
	¼ teaspoon salt

In mixing bowl, place butter, shallots, garlic, basil, anchovies, lemon juice, pepper, and salt and blend on #6 speed until well combined. Makes about 1⅓ cups.

A fairly smooth butter flecked with anchovy and shallots. For a tasty canapé, spread it on Italian bread rounds and bake or serve over cooked broccoli, cauliflower, baked potatoes, or pasta. Try spreading on toasts to serve atop fish stew, bouillabaise, and the like.

GREEN CHILI BUTTER

1 can (4-ounce/114-mL) green chilies, drained and chopped	1 large garlic clove, minced
½ cup butter, at room temperature	4 green onions, chopped (green part only)
½ cup (4 ounces) cream cheese, at room temperature	1 teaspoon dried oregano
	¼ teaspoon salt

In mixing bowl, place chilies, butter, cream cheese, garlic, green onions, oregano, and salt. Blend on #6 speed until combined. It will be a textured butter. Makes about 1½ cups.

Lots of pizzazz in this butter. Wonderful on warm corn bread or corn muffins. Try it as a spread on tortilla chips or as a zippy butter for boiled corn, green beans, new potatoes, or fish.

Apple Flan with Creme Chantilly
(page 185)

APPLE BUTTER

8 cups apple cider	1 cup brown sugar
3 pounds Granny Smith	1 tablespoon fresh lemon juice
apples, peeled, cored, and	1 teaspoon ground cloves
quartered	1 teaspoon ground cinnamon
1 pound McIntosh apples,	1 teaspoon ground allspice
peeled, cored, and	½ teaspoon powdered ginger
quartered	

In heavy 3-quart saucepan, over high heat, boil cider, uncovered, until reduced by half, about 30 minutes. Stir in apples, sugar, lemon juice, cloves, cinnamon, allspice, and ginger. Reduce heat to low and cook for about 40 minutes, stirring, or until thickened. Blend on #6 speed in saucepan for 30 seconds. Continue cooking over medium-high heat, if necessary, to thicken. Cool before serving. Makes about 5½ cups.

Serve alongside pork, ham, or sausages or spread on toast, muffins, pound cake, or waffles.

Apple Butter (recipe this page)
with muffins

ANCHOVY BUTTER

6 anchovy fillets, drained and chopped	½ cup butter, at room temperature
Freshly ground black pepper	

In mixing bowl, place anchovies and pepper to taste. Add butter gradually and blend on #6 speed until smooth. Makes about ½ cup.

Stir a little of this butter into osso bucco (braised veal shanks, Milan style). Spread on pita bread and build mini pizzas. It's also delicious swirled into spinach or carrot soup.

REALLY GREEN SNAIL BUTTER

½ cup butter, at room temperature	2 tablespoons fresh lemon juice
	1 teaspoon dried thyme
2 green onions, minced	1 teaspoon dried tarragon
4 large garlic cloves, minced	1 teaspoon dried basil
1 shallot, minced	¼ teaspoon freshly ground
¼ cup chopped fresh parsley	black pepper

In mixing bowl, place butter, green onions, garlic, shallot, parsley, lemon juice, thyme, tarragon, basil, and pepper. Blend on #6 speed until well combined. Makes about ⅔ cup butter.

Stuff snail shells with snails and butter or melt butter mixture in a skillet and add drained snails; cook 5 minutes or until hot and bubbly. Serve immediately with lots of crusty bread. Enough butter for 8 ounces (250-g) snails.

CAPER BUTTER

½ cup butter, at room temperature	1 tablespoon minced fresh parsley
3 tablespoons capers	1 tablespoon fresh lemon juice
1 tablespoon finely chopped green onion (green part only)	⅛ teaspoon freshly ground black pepper

In mixing bowl, place butter, capers, green onion, parsley, lemon juice, and pepper; blend on #6 speed until combined. Butter will have a coarse texture. Makes about ¾ cup.

Caper lovers will enjoy this butter over pasta. Baste chicken breasts or grilled fish with it while cooking or melt it to serve as a sauce for either. Make tuna sandwiches sing with this butter spread on the bread, kaisers, or what-you-will.

GOAT CHEESE AND SUN-DRIED TOMATO SPREAD

¼ cup butter, at room temperature	*½ teaspoon red pepper flakes, or to taste*
5 ounces goat cheese, at room temperature	*4 sun-dried tomatoes in olive oil, drained and minced*
Finely grated zest of 1 large orange	

In mixing bowl, blend butter, cheese, orange zest, red pepper flakes, and sun-dried tomatoes on #6 speed until smooth and well combined. Makes about 1 cup.

Fabulous marriage of orange, goat cheese, and sun-dried tomatoes. Stuff boned chicken breasts with the butter, roll in a crumb or nut coating, and bake. Also very tasty spread on toasted bagels or crackers.

CRAB MOUSSE

1 package gelatin	1 small onion, minced
¼ cup cold water	2 cans (each 4.5-ounce/128-g)
1 can (10-ounce/284-mL)	crabmeat, drained
cream of mushroom soup	¼ teaspoon freshly ground
1 cup (8 ounces) cream cheese	white pepper
¾ cup mayonnaise	Garnish:
2 tablespoons chopped fresh dill	Fresh dill sprigs
⅛ teaspoon Tabasco	Lemon slices
1 stalk celery, minced	

In small bowl, sprinkle gelatin over water. Set aside to dissolve.

In large heavy saucepan or Dutch oven, stir in mushroom soup, cream cheese, mayonnaise, dill, and Tabasco; simmer over medium-low heat for 2 minutes or until smooth. Remove from heat. Add gelatin and blend on #6 speed until smooth. Return to medium-low heat; simmer, stirring, until gelatin is completely dissolved. Stir in celery, onion, crabmeat, and pepper; pour into well-oiled 5-cup mold; chill overnight. Alternately, line an 8½ x 4½-inch loaf pan with plastic wrap; pour mixture into prepared pan, smoothing surface with spatula. Garnish with dill sprigs and lemon slices. Serves 8.

Serve this creamy-white, delicate-tasting mousse with plain water biscuits.

SMOKED TROUT MOUSSE

1 7-ounce smoked rainbow trout, skinned, filleted and deboned (about 1 cup flaked trout, loosely packed)	Grated zest of 1 lemon 2 teaspoons fresh lemon juice ½ cup (4 ounces) cream cheese, at room temperature
1 tablespoon prepared hot horseradish	¼ teaspoon Tabasco 1 tablespoon chopped fresh dill
1 tablespoon heavy cream	

In mixing bowl, blend flaked trout, horseradish, cream, lemon zest, and lemon juice on #6 speed until well combined. Gradually add cream cheese, Tabasco, and dill; blend until smooth. Makes about 1 cup.

The tang of lemon and smoky trout flavor make this mousse fabulous on crackers, with crudités, or piped into cherry tomatoes, Belgian endive, or radicchio leaves, then garnished on a platter with dill sprigs and lemon wedges.

ASPARAGUS TOASTS

1 cup blue cheese (about 5 ounces), at room temperature	*1 loaf fresh white sandwich bread, crusts removed*
1 cup (8 ounces) cream cheese, at room temperature	*1 loaf fresh whole-wheat sandwich bread, crusts removed*
Grated zest of 1 small orange	*1 cup butter, melted*
Pinch red pepper flakes	*1½ cups sesame seeds, lightly toasted*
36 thin fresh asparagus spears	

In mixing bowl, blend blue cheese, cream cheese, orange zest, and red pepper flakes on #6 speed until mixture is smooth. Set aside.

Steam asparagus until tender, refresh under cold water to cool; drain and dry well.

Flatten bread slices with rolling pin. Spread cheese mixture thinly on bread slices. Place an asparagus spear at bottom of each slice, roll tightly, and pinch seams together. Brush generously with melted butter and roll in sesame seeds on a plate. Trim away any spears that protrude from end of rolls.

Place on baking sheet and bake in 450°F oven for 10 to 15 minutes or until thoroughly toasted. (If too lightly toasted, the flavor is bland, but take care not to burn either!) Remove from oven and let toasts stand for 2 minutes on baking sheet. Slice in half before serving. Makes 36 rolls or 72 pieces.

Served warm, these toasts are a surprise in flavor with the asparagus-blue cheese combination. They are great as an appetizer and also particularly good served alongside a bowl of hearty soup. The bread must be absolutely fresh in order to pinch seams together. I use the two different breads for color contrast, but try all white or all whole-wheat if you prefer. These can be made up ahead, frozen between sheets of wax paper, and baked frozen.

CHEESE DREAMS
(CHEDDAR CHEESE SPREAD)

1 pound bacon, cut into ½-inch pieces	2 tablespoons light or heavy cream
1 cup (8 ounces) nippy or old Cheddar cheese spread, at room temperature	1 tablespoon mayonnaise
	1 teaspoon Dijon mustard
	¼ teaspoon freshly ground black pepper
¼ cup butter, at room temperature	1 loaf sliced sandwich bread, crusts removed

In skillet, fry bacon until beginning to crisp. Remove to a paper-towel-lined plate to drain.

In mixing bowl, blend cheese, butter, cream, mayonnaise, mustard, and pepper on #6 speed until smooth.

Place trimmed bread slices on baking sheet. Broil until lightly toasted on one side. Turn over and spread cheese mixture on untoasted side. Place bacon on top of cheese mixture and broil until bacon is crisp, about 2 minutes. Remove from oven and cut each bread slice in half diagonally. Makes 2¼ cups cheese spread and 36 triangles.

These make appetizing snacks or lunch bites. For petite savories to serve with cocktails, cut each slice into 4 triangles. If you wish to omit the bacon, spread cheese mixture on untoasted bread slices; roll the slices and bake until toasted. Cut in half to serve. Try spooning this nippy cheese mixutre into croustade cases or into crustless sandwich bread that has been sliced in half, brushed with melted butter, pressed into tiny tart tins, and baked until toasted for a pointed croustade case. The spread makes a colorful, flavorful topping for baked potatoes. Store spread in refrigerator for up to one week; use as needed.

FRESH DILL DIP

½ cup (4 ounces) cream cheese, at room temperature	2 tablespoons fresh chopped dill
½ cup mayonnaise	¼ teaspoon freshly ground black pepper
½ cup light sour cream	
2 green onions, minced	

In mixing bowl, blend cream cheese, mayonnaise, and sour cream on #6 speed until combined. Add green onions, dill, and pepper; blend again until combined. Makes about 1⅔ cups.

Fresh-tasting dip for crudités; top or stuff baked potatoes with this dip, or serve on grilled swordfish or salmon.

CHICKPEA DIP

1 can (19-ounce/540-mL)	2 garlic cloves, minced
chickpeas, drained	1 tablespoon mayonnaise
¼ cup olive oil	2 tablespoons fresh lemon
¼ cup finely chopped	juice
red onion	½ teaspoon salt
¼ cup finely chopped	Freshly ground black pepper
fresh parsley	

In mixing bowl, blend chickpeas, oil, onion, parsley, garlic, mayonnaise, lemon juice, salt, and pepper to taste on #6 speed until well combined. Do not overblend; this dip should be smooth, but still have some texture. Makes 1¾ cups.

I love this garlicky, lemony-flavored dip. Garnish with chopped parsley or coriander and a drizzle of olive oil. Wonderful served with warm pita bread triangles, crackers (preferably plain water crackers), or with an assortment of raw vegetables. Try miniature pita halves stuffed with dip and a little leaf lettuce as an hors d'oeuvre.

CREAMY CURRY DIP

1 tablespoon vegetable oil	*½ cup tomato or tomato-*
3 tablespoons finely chopped	*clam juice*
shallots	*2 tablespoons apricot jam or*
1 tablespoon curry powder	*chutney*
1 teaspoon paprika	*1 cup mayonnaise*

In medium saucepan, heat oil over medium heat. Add shallots; cook, stirring, for 3 minutes or until tender. Add curry and paprika; cook, stirring, for 1 minute. Add tomato juice and jam; blend occasionally on #3 speed for 7 minutes or until thickened. Cool completely; blend in mayonnaise. Makes about 1½ cups.

Serve over poached fish or use as a dipping sauce for cooked cold shrimp or crudités.

ROASTED RED PEPPER DIP

2 sweet red peppers, roasted, peeled, seeded, and chopped	2 tablespoons chopped fresh parsley
½ cup sour cream	1 tablespoon chopped fresh
½ cup plain yogurt	thyme or ½ teaspoon dried
1 teaspoon fresh lemon juice	1 tablespoon chopped fresh basil

In mixing bowl, blend peppers, sour cream, yogurt, lemon juice, parsley, thyme, and basil on #6 speed until well combined. Makes about 2 cups.

A beautiful autumn red color, this dip tastes divine. Roasting the peppers brings out a smoky sweetness. Serve as a dip with snow peas and asparagus or as a sauce with cold roast beef or filet of beef.
*To roast red pepper, place whole pepper on baking sheet. Broil, turning frequently, for about 20 minutes or until skin is blackened. Remove from oven; let cool. Peel, halve, and remove seeds.

GREEN CHILI DIP

2 cans (each 4-ounce/114-mL)	⅓ cup sour cream
green chilies, drained and	¼ teaspoon salt
chopped	⅛ teaspoon chili powder, or
4 green onions, chopped	to taste
1 tomato, seeded and chopped	Garnish:
½ cup (4 ounces) cream	Fresh coriander or parsley,
cheese, at room temperature	chopped

In mixing bowl, blend chilies, green onions, tomato, cream cheese, sour cream, salt, and chili powder to taste on #6 speed until well combined but not smooth. Garnish with chopped fresh coriander. Makes about 2 cups.

A spicy dip for crudités or corn chips. When blending, leave some texture in mixture for interest.

CHUTNEY CURRY CREAM CHEESE DIP

*1 cup (8 ounces) cream
cheese, at room temperature*

*½ cup chutney
1 tablespoon curry powder*

In mixing bowl, blend cream cheese, chutney, and curry powder on #6 speed until combined. This spread will not be smooth. Makes about 1½ cups.

Serve with raw carrots, celery, fennel, radishes, cauliflower, or any other crunchy fresh vegetable.

FETA ANCHOVY DIP

1 cup (about 4 ounces) crumbled feta cheese, at room temperature	4 green onions, finely chopped
	¼ teaspoon Tabasco
	¼ teaspoon freshly ground
¼ cup (2 ounces) cream cheese, at room temperature	black pepper
	2 tablespoons chopped fresh
¼ cup sour cream	parsley
1 can (1.75-ounce/50-g) anchovy fillets, drained	

In mixing bowl, blend feta cheese, cream cheese, sour cream, anchovies, green onions, Tabasco, and pepper on #6 speed until well combined. Chill, covered, several hours for flavors to blend. Remove from refrigerator; bring to room temperature. Sprinkle with chopped parsley. Makes about 1 cup.

Serve with crispy poppadums, toasted pita points, shellfish such as shrimp or your favorite vegetable dippers.

HOT CRAB AND CHEESE DIP

½ cup butter	2¼ cups fresh, frozen,* or
5 large garlic cloves, minced	canned crabmeat (3 cans,
3 cups (about 12 ounces)	each 4.5-ounce/128-g)
grated Swiss or Cheddar	2 green onions, minced
cheese	¼ teaspoon freshly ground
¼ cup light cream	black pepper
1 tablespoon dry sherry	
1 teaspoon Tabasco, or to taste	

In heavy saucepan or enamel fondue pot, melt butter over low heat. Add garlic and cook, stirring, for 2 minutes. Add cheese, cream, sherry, and Tabasco to taste. In saucepan, over low heat, blend on #5 speed until combined. Stir in crabmeat, green onions, and pepper. Cook until crabmeat is heated through. Serve warm with crackers, celery sticks, or crusty bread. Serves 4.

Very rich — but worth the calories! Great cocktail party fare. Serve in patty shells for appetizers. Fill crepes with crab fondue and serve at brunch. Or use vegetable crudités as a dipper.

*Note: if using frozen crabmeat, thaw and squeeze dry before cooking.

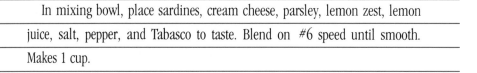

SARDINE SPREAD

1 can (3.5-ounce/100-g)	2 tablespoons fresh lemon
sardines in tomato sauce,	juice
undrained	¼ teaspoon salt
½ cup (4 ounces) cream	¼ teaspoon freshly ground
cheese, at room temperature	black pepper
¼ cup minced fresh parsley	Few drops Tabasco
Grated zest of 1 lemon	

In mixing bowl, place sardines, cream cheese, parsley, lemon zest, lemon juice, salt, pepper, and Tabasco to taste. Blend on #6 speed until smooth. Makes 1 cup.

Spread on crackers, bread, or warm pitas or serve as a dip for crudités.

AVOCADO DIP

1 ripe avocado, peeled and cubed	3 tablespoons chopped fresh parsley
1 tomato, seeded and chopped	3 tablespoons chopped fresh coriander
2 tablespoons fresh lemon juice	2 tablespoons sour cream
2 large garlic cloves, minced	Salt
2 green onions, minced	Freshly ground black pepper

In mixing bowl, place avocado, tomato, lemon juice, garlic, green onions, parsley, 2 tablespoons coriander, sour cream, salt, and pepper. Blend on #4 speed until just combined. Do not overblend. Some texture should be visible — it should be a bit chunky. Garnish with remaining chopped coriander. Serve immediately, as this dip will darken in color if it stands. Makes about 1½ cups.

A pretty and tangy dip to serve with corn chips, fresh vegetables, or pita toasts. Great, too, on a baked potato or in a pita pocket.

CHAPTER TWO

SWEET AND SAVORY SAUCES AND DRESSINGS

MAYONNAISE I

MAYONNAISE II

LIME MAYONNAISE

ROASTED RED PEPPER MAYONNAISE

AIOLI (GARLIC MAYONNAISE)

SESAME DRESSING

VERY LEMON VINAIGRETTE

CAESAR DRESSING

BASIL VINAIGRETTE

THOUSAND ISLAND DRESSING

AVOCADO DRESSING

BLUE CHEESE DRESSING

CREAMY RED WINE VINAIGRETTE

CREAMY CUCUMBER DRESSING

TARRAGON SESAME DRESSING

CREAMY GARLIC DRESSING

GREEN GODDESS DRESSING

HONEY DRESSING

LOW-CAL BUTTERMILK HERB DRESSING

CREAMY PARMESAN DRESSING

BEURRE BLANC

HOLLANDAISE

JEZEBEL SAUCE

BÉARNAISE SAUCE

CHICKEN GRAVY

HOT 'N' SPICY PEANUT SAUCE

RASPBERRY SAUCE

GRANNY SMITH APPLESAUCE

LIGHT CHOCOLATE SAUCE

MAYONNAISE I

2 large egg yolks	¼ teaspoon salt
2 tablespoons fresh lemon	¼ teaspoon freshly ground
juice, or to taste	black pepper
2 tablespoons Dijon mustard	1 to 1½ cups olive or
⅛ teaspoon cayenne	vegetable oil

In beaker, place egg yolks, lemon juice, mustard, cayenne, salt, pepper, and oil. Place blender flat against bottom of beaker. Blend on #6 speed for about 20 seconds; guide blender to top of mixture and back down again. Do not raise blade out of mixture while blending. Makes about 1¼ to 1¾ cups.

This mayonnaise has a thicker consistency than the following recipe. A teaspoon of dried tarragon adds a nice flavor to it. Or add other herbs plus a little minced garlic. Try flavored vinegars in place of lemon juice for a nice change.

MAYONNAISE II

1 extra-large egg	¼ teaspoon freshly ground
3 teaspoons fresh lemon juice	black pepper
1 teaspoon Dijon mustard	1 cup olive oil or
½ teaspoon dry mustard	vegetable oil
¼ teaspoon salt	

In beaker, place egg, lemon juice, mustards, salt, pepper, and oil. Place blender flat against bottom of beaker. Blend on #6 speed for about 20 seconds; guide blender to top of mixture and back down again. Do not raise blade out of mixture while blending. Makes about 1¼ cups.

It is important to keep blender over egg yolk when making mayonnaise or it will not emulsify properly. This is a thinner mayonnaise than the previous recipe. There is nothing like homemade mayonnaise to spread on bread for sandwiches, or to use as the base of your favorite cole slaw. Add a little chopped pimento or some minced fresh herbs such as parsley or chives.

LIME MAYONNAISE

1 extra-large egg	¼ teaspoon freshly ground
Finely grated zest of 2 limes	black pepper
4 teaspoons lime juice	⅛ teaspoon cayenne
2 teaspoons Dijon mustard	⅛ teaspoon dried mint
¼ teaspoon salt	1 cup vegetable oil

In beaker, place egg, lime zest, lime juice, mustard, salt, pepper, cayenne, mint, and oil. Place blender flat against bottom of beaker. Blend on #6 speed for about 20 seconds; guide blender to top of mixture and back down again. Do not raise blade out of mixture while blending. Makes about 1¼ cups.

This mayonnaise is light in consistency and smacks of tangy lime flavor. Serve with cooked lobster, shrimp, or grilled swordfish steaks — any fish eaten at room temperature. Add a bit of the exotic to your next tuna-fish sandwich by spreading whole-grain bread with this mayonnaise. How about potato-salad with a Caribbean accent? Or curried chicken salad using this mayo?

ROASTED RED PEPPER MAYONNAISE

4 extra-large egg yolks	1 teaspoon dry mustard
2 tablespoons fresh lemon	1 teaspoon salt
juice	¾ teaspoon freshly ground
1 tablespoon tarragon vinegar	black pepper
1 sweet red pepper, roasted	1 cup olive oil
and finely chopped	¾ cup vegetable oil
2 teaspoons Dijon mustard	

In beaker, place egg yolks, lemon juice, vinegar, red pepper, mustards, salt, pepper, and oils. Place blender flat against bottom of beaker. Blend on #6 speed for about 20 seconds; guide blender to top of mixture and back down again. Do not raise blade out of mixture while blending. Makes about 2½ cups.

Delicious with poached salmon trout or rare filet of beef or lamb. Wonderful as a spread for the base of canapés; spread mayonnaise on fresh baked bread and place rare roast beef or thinly sliced chicken on top. This can also be piped into hollowed-out cherry tomatoes for an hors d'oeuvre.

AIOLI (GARLIC MAYONNAISE)

4 extra-large egg yolks	1 teaspoon salt
2 tablespoons Dijon mustard	1 teaspoon freshly ground
6 garlic cloves, minced	black pepper
2 tablespoons fresh lemon juice	¾ cup olive oil
3 teaspoons dry mustard	¾ cup vegetable oil

In beaker, place egg yolks, Dijon mustard, garlic, lemon juice, dry mustard, salt, pepper, and oils. Place blender flat against bottom of beaker. Blend on #6 speed for about 20 seconds; guide blender to top of mixture and back down again. Do not raise blade out of mixture while blending. Mixture should be thick. Makes about 1¾ cups.

This garlicky mayonnaise from Provence in southern France is often called "the butter of Provence", "the soul of the South", or "the butter of the sun". It is traditionally served with an array of meats, fish, snails, salt cod, eggs, and raw and cooked vegetables. I like to serve it with a platter of warm steamed new potatoes, green beans, beets, radishes, fennel, and salmon along with warm French bread and a robust red wine. It's wonderful simply as a dip for vegetables and cold seafood.

SESAME DRESSING

½ cup vegetable oil	1 large egg yolk
¼ teaspoon rice wine vinegar	1 teaspoon dry mustard
2 tablespoons sesame oil	1 teaspoon sugar
2 tablespoons soy sauce	¼ teaspoon cayenne

In beaker, blend oil, vinegar, sesame oil, soy sauce, egg yolk, mustard, sugar, and cayenne on #6 speed until smooth and emulsified. Makes about 1 cup.

Add a delicious oriental touch to marinated vegetables with this dressing. Adapt an oriental salad of chopped cucumber, green onion, radishes, coriander, and cooked shrimp; spoon onto a nest of bean sprouts and drizzle sesame dressing over top. Sprinkle with toasted sesame seeds.

ॐ

VERY LEMON VINAIGRETTE

1½ cups vegetable oil	1 teaspoon salt
⅓ cup fresh lemon juice	Freshly ground black pepper

In beaker, blend oil, lemon juice, salt, and pepper to taste on #4 speed for about 20 seconds or until emulsified and smooth. Makes about 1¾ cups.

Very light, yet very tangy. Serve with a selection of lettuces such as romaine, radicchio, red-leaf, Belgian endive, and arugula. Try marinating cauliflower florets in this vinaigrette, then tossing them with lots of fresh watercress and cherry tomatoes. Also tasty over poached leeks or asparagus.

CAESAR DRESSING

1 cup olive oil	1 tablespoon Dijon mustard
6 to 8 anchovy fillets, drained	1 tablespoon red wine vinegar
Juice of 1 lemon	1 tablespoon Worcestershire
2 to 3 large garlic cloves,	sauce
minced	¼ teaspoon salt
1 extra-large egg	¼ teaspoon freshly ground
3 tablespoons freshly grated	black pepper
Parmesan cheese	

In beaker, place oil, anchovies, lemon juice, garlic, egg, Parmesan cheese, mustard, vinegar, Worcestershire sauce, salt, and pepper. Blend on #6 speed until well combined and thickened. Makes about 2 cups.

Good and garlicky. Toss over 1 large head romaine lettuce, washed and torn; add crumbled cooked bacon and homemade croutons.

BASIL VINAIGRETTE

½ cup vegetable oil	1 tablespoon Dijon mustard
½ cup olive oil	½ teaspoon salt
¼ cup fresh lemon juice	½ teaspoon freshly ground
¼ cup chopped fresh basil or	black pepper
1 tablespoon dried	

In beaker, blend oils, lemon juice, basil, mustard, salt, and pepper. Blend on #4 speed for about 20 seconds or until emulsified and smooth. Makes about 1⅓ cups.

There is nothing like a fresh garden salad to accept a showering of basil vinaigrette. Great tossed with cooked pasta as a base for pasta salad. Toss in chopped tomatoes, black olives, and feta cheese for a Greek touch. This is wonderful for tomato salads with black olives, mozzarella cheese, and capers, or try it tossed with a red onion and anchovy salad, or over a green bean and red pepper salad.

Basil Vinaigrette (recipe this page)
with tomato salad

THOUSAND ISLAND DRESSING

1 cup mayonnaise	1 tablespoon chopped fresh
¼ cup finely chopped sweet	parsley
red pepper	¼ teaspoon salt
2 tablespoons chili sauce	¼ teaspoon freshly ground
2 green onions, chopped	black pepper

In bowl, blend mayonnaise, red pepper, chili sauce, green onion, parsley, salt, and pepper on #5 speed until combined. Chill 3 to 4 hours before serving. Makes about 1¼ cups.

Serve over iceberg lettuce or spread on rye bread and build a thick Reuben sandwich.

*Thousand Island Dressing (recipe this page)
and Green Goddess Dressing (page 76)*

AVOCADO DRESSING

2 small (about 14 ounces)	½ cup plain yogurt
ripe avocados, peeled and	¼ cup vegetable oil
chopped	1 tablespoon fresh lemon juice
1 small onion, finely chopped	Salt
1 large garlic clove, minced	Freshly ground black pepper

In mixing bowl, place avocado, onion, garlic, yogurt, oil, lemon juice, salt, and pepper to taste. Blend on #6 speed until smooth.

A delicious, pale-green, creamy dressing that is thick enough to use as a dip too! Very tasty over a taco-salad — tortillas mounded with shredded lettuce, cheese, and chopped tomatoes. Stuff a pita with thinly-sliced steak, shredded lettuce, chopped tomatoes, and this dressing.

BLUE CHEESE DRESSING

¾ cup (about 3 ounces)	1 tablespoon red wine vinegar
crumbled blue cheese	2 garlic cloves, minced
½ cup light sour cream	¼ teaspoon salt
2 tablespoons mayonnaise	¼ teaspoon freshly ground
2 tablespoons olive oil	black pepper

In beaker, blend ½ cup blue cheese, sour cream, mayonnaise, oil, vinegar, garlic, salt, and pepper on #4 speed until combined. Crumble remaining cheese on top of salad. Makes about 1 cup.

Serve over crisp iceberg or romaine lettuce with chopped green onions and tomato quarters. Another idea is to spread on French stick and layer rare roast beef, lettuce, and radish slices on top.

CREAMY RED WINE VINAIGRETTE

1 cup vegetable oil	1 teaspoon Dijon mustard
¼ cup red wine vinegar	Salt
1 extra-large egg	Freshly ground black pepper

In beaker, blend oil, vinegar, egg mustard, salt, and pepper to taste on #4 speed until emulsified and thickened slightly. Makes about 1¼ cups.

Drizzle over thinly-sliced fresh summer tomatoes with lots of chopped fresh basil, mint, or dill sprinkled on top. Superb tossed with grated zucchini and chopped fresh basil. A platter of fresh fennel slices arranged on leaf lettuce and sprinkled liberally with this dressing is a very refreshing side dish on a hot summer evening.

CREAMY CUCUMBER DRESSING

1 cup peeled and diced	1 garlic clove, minced
English cucumber	1 tablespoon chopped fresh
½ cup plain yogurt	dill
½ cup light sour cream	¼ teaspoon salt
3 green onions, chopped	¼ teaspoon freshly ground
	pepper

In beaker, blend cucumber, yogurt, sour cream, onions, garlic, dill, salt, and pepper on #6 speed until combined. Chill before serving. Makes about 2 cups.

A cool, creamy-white dressing with green flecks throughout. Make it low-cal by using skim milk yogurt and light sour cream.

TARRAGON SESAME DRESSING

¼ cup vegetable oil	½ teaspoon sesame oil
2 tablespoons tarragon	¼ teaspoon dried tarragon
vinegar	¼ teaspoon freshly ground
2 tablespoons liquid honey	black pepper
½ teaspoon salt	¼ cup sesame seeds, toasted

In beaker, blend oil, vinegar, honey, salt, sesame oil, tarragon, and pepper on #5 speed until thickened. Stir in sesame seeds. Makes about ⅔ cup.

I like to serve this dressing over cooked and cooled buckwheat noodles, sprinkled with chopped green onions, coarsely chopped water chestnuts, julienned carrots, shredded spinach, and fresh bean sprouts. Why not try your own oriental-inspired salad? Sprinkle sesame seeds on top instead of incorporating in dressing.

CREAMY GARLIC DRESSING

¼ cup olive or vegetable oil	2 tablespoons chopped fresh
½ large egg yolk	parsley
2 tablespoons red wine	¼ teaspoon salt
vinegar	¼ teaspoon freshly ground
1 tablespoon Dijon mustard	black pepper
2 medium garlic cloves,	
minced	

In beaker, place oil, egg yolk, vinegar, mustard, garlic, parsley, salt, and pepper; blend on #6 speed until thickened. Be careful not to overblend or it will thicken too much. Makes about ½ cup.

Toss this piquant dressing over steamed green beans, asparagus, or braised leeks. Or with 1/2 head romaine lettuce and ripe summer tomatoes.

GREEN GODDESS DRESSING

1 cup mayonnaise	1 tablespoon chopped fresh
6 anchovy fillets, drained	parsley
and chopped	1 teaspoon dried tarragon
5 green onions, chopped	¼ teaspoon salt
1 tablespoon fresh lemon	¼ teaspoon freshly ground
juice	black pepper

In beaker, blend mayonnaise, anchovies, green onions, lemon juice, parsley, tarragon, salt, and pepper on #6 speed until combined. Chill before serving. Makes 1⅓ cups.

This classic American dressing is quite thick and is delicious on seafood salads or on romaine lettuce. Mix it with tuna or salmon for sandwiches, or serve with baked potatoes. A good dip for crudités.

HONEY DRESSING

1 cup vegetable oil	1 teaspoon dry mustard
¼ cup red wine vinegar	1 teaspoon celery seed
2 tablespoons liquid honey	¼ teaspoon paprika
1 tablespoon sugar	¼ teaspoon salt
1 small onion, finely chopped	¼ teaspoon freshly ground
1 tablespoon fresh lemon juice	black pepper

In beaker, place oil, vinegar, honey, sugar, onion, lemon juice, mustard, celery seed, paprika, salt, and pepper; blend on #5 speed until well combined. Makes about 1⅔ cups.

Wonderful on fruit salads or on a salad of romaine lettuce and crumbled blue cheese. Even spinach salad with orange segments would marry well with this dressing. Or papaya and avocado slices with thinly sliced red onion on a bed of shredded leaf lettuce.

LOW-CAL BUTTERMILK HERB DRESSING

1 cup buttermilk	*1 tablespoon chopped fresh*
½ cup low-cal plain yogurt	*summer savory or*
1 tablespoon low-cal	*½ teaspoon dried*
mayonnaise	*1 tablespoon chopped fresh*
2 tablespoons snipped fresh	*mint or ½ teaspoon dried*
chives	*¼ teaspoon salt*
1 garlic clove, minced	*¼ teaspoon freshly ground*
1 tablespoon chopped fresh	*black pepper*
dill or ½ teaspoon dried	

In beaker, blend buttermilk, yogurt, mayonnaise, chives, garlic, dill, summer savory, mint, salt, and pepper on #5 speed until combined. Chill before serving. Makes about 1⅔ cups.

If possible, use all fresh herbs for a lovely garden-fresh taste.

CREAMY PARMESAN DRESSING

½ cup olive oil	1 tablespoon Dijon mustard
1 egg yolk	1 garlic clove, minced
¼ cup freshly grated	¼ teaspoon dried oregano
Parmesan cheese	¼ teaspoon salt
2 tablespoons red wine	¼ teaspoon freshly ground
vinegar	black pepper
1 tablespoon fresh	
lemon juice	

In beaker, blend oil, egg yolk, Parmesan, vinegar, lemon juice, mustard, garlic, oregano, salt, and pepper on #6 speed until thickened. Makes about 1 cup.

This dressing is similar to Caesar Salad Dressing — milder and less pungent — but very tasty.

BEURRE BLANC

2 tablespoons minced shallots	¼ teaspoon freshly ground
½ cup dry white vermouth	white pepper
¼ cup tarragon vinegar	1 cup butter, cut into small
1 tablespoon fresh lemon juice	pieces, at room temperature
¼ teaspoon salt	

In heavy medium saucepan, cook shallots, vermouth, vinegar, lemon juice, salt, and pepper over high heat for 30 minutes or until reduced to 2 tablespoons. Remove saucepan from heat; gradually add butter, blending on #3 speed constantly until incorporated. Transfer to warm serving bowl. Makes about 1 cup.

A creamy, golden-brown buttery sauce to serve with fish. It is important to blend in butter off the heat, so that sauce does not turn oily.

HOLLANDAISE SAUCE

2 extra-large egg yolks	Freshly ground white pepper
1 tablespoon fresh lemon juice	½ cup butter, cut into small
Pinch cayenne	pieces
Salt	

In top of double boiler, over hot but not boiling water, blend egg yolks, lemon juice, cayenne, salt, and pepper to taste on #6 speed until combined. Add butter gradually, blending constantly on #6 speed, until sauce thickens, about 1 to 2 minutes. Makes about ⅔ cup.

Serve buttery hollandaise over cooked vegetables such as asparagus or cauliflower. Traditional with eggs benedict or fish.

JEZEBEL SAUCE

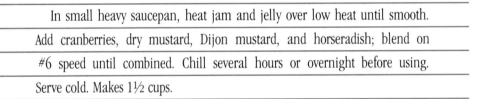

½ cup pineapple jam	1 tablespoon dry mustard
½ cup red currant jelly	1 tablespoon Dijon mustard
1 cup fresh or thawed frozen	1 tablespoon prepared hot
cranberries	horseradish

In small heavy saucepan, heat jam and jelly over low heat until smooth. Add cranberries, dry mustard, Dijon mustard, and horseradish; blend on #6 speed until combined. Chill several hours or overnight before using. Serve cold. Makes 1½ cups.

A beautiful, rosy-cranberry-colored sauce to serve with hot or cold turkey, chicken, or goose.

BÉARNAISE SAUCE

3 shallots, finely chopped	3 extra-large egg yolks
3 tablespoons tarragon vinegar	1 tablespoon fresh lemon
1 tablespoon dried tarragon	juice
½ cup dry white vermouth	¼ teaspoon freshly
1 cup butter, cubed	ground black pepper
	Pinch cayenne

In beaker, blend egg yolks, lemon juice, pepper, and cayenne on #6 speed for 40 seconds. Pour in foaming hot butter. Blend on #6 speed until sauce is thickened. Makes about 1⅓ cups.

Sublime on broiled or grilled meats and fish or eggs. You can freeze béarnaise sauce and use as a compound butter, to enhance poached, baked, or grilled fish and baked potatoes.

CHICKEN GRAVY

⅓ cup butter	*3 cups chicken stock*
¼ cup all-purpose flour	*¼ teaspoon salt*
¼ teaspoon dried sage	*¼ teaspoon freshly ground*
¼ teaspoon dried thyme	*black pepper*

In medium saucepan, melt butter over medium high heat. Remove from heat. Add flour; stir, using wooden spoon until combined. Return saucepan to heat; cook, stirring, for about 3 minutes or until flour and butter begin to have a nutty aroma. Remove saucepan from heat. Add chicken stock, sage, thyme, salt, and pepper; blend on #3 speed until combined. Return saucepan to heat and cook for about 5 minutes, or until thickened. Makes about 2½ cups.

Serve with french fries, roasted potatoes, fried chicken, or over a hot chicken sandwich.

HOT 'N' SPICY PEANUT SAUCE

1 tablespoon vegetable oil	3 tablespoons fresh lemon
1 large onion, chopped	juice
2 large garlic cloves, minced	3 tablespoons liquid honey
½ cup peanut butter	1 tablespoon soy sauce
¼ cup dry white vermouth	2 teaspoons sambal oelek* or
3 tablespoons sweet chili sauce	chili paste with soy bean*

In heavy medium saucepan, heat oil over medium heat. Add onion and garlic; cook for 5 minutes or until soft. Stir in peanut butter, vermouth, chili sauce, lemon juice, honey, soy sauce, and sambal oelek. Reduce heat to low; blend on #6 speed until ingredients are well combined. Makes 1½ cups.

An excellent dip, bursting with flavor, to serve with pork, chicken, or beef satay. Great as a dip for crudités or brochettes, too.

**Note: Sambal oelek is an Indonesian red chili condiment available in Dutch or Oriental markets. Chili paste with soy bean is a Chinese hot sauce available in Chinese grocery stores.

RASPBERRY SAUCE

½ cup sugar	1 package (10-ounce/300-g)
½ cup water	frozen unsweetened
Finely grated zest of	raspberries, thawed
1 grapefruit	

In medium saucepan, bring sugar, water, and zest to a boil; cook, uncovered, for 10 to 15 minutes, or until syrup thickens. Brush down sides of saucepan with water occasionally to prevent crystallization. Add raspberries to syrup and blend in saucepan on #6 speed until combined. Strain through a sieve to remove seeds. Makes about 1¼ cups.

A brilliant red sauce. Cover the center of a large plate with sauce and create a gorgeous palette using fresh fruits. Dust with icing sugar. Serve over ice cream, crème brûlée, pound cake, or pancakes. You can substitute frozen strawberries for raspberries. This sauce can be frozen.

GRANNY SMITH APPLESAUCE

6 pounds Granny Smith	Juice of 1 lemon
apples, peeled, cored,	½ cup sugar
and quartered	½ teaspoon cinnamon
1 cup water	(optional)

In heavy saucepan over medium heat, simmer apples, water, and lemon juice, covered. Cook for about 25 minutes or until very tender, stirring occasionally. Blend on #4 speed until puréed. Add sugar and cook over low heat until sugar is dissolved. Stir in cinnamon if using and remove from heat. Serve warm or refrigerate until needed. Makes about 8 cups.

Tart and not too sweet. Serve with pork chops, roast pork, or stuffed pork tenderloin. Make an applesauce cake using your favorite recipe and this apple purée. Also tasty with a slice of Cheddar cheese and biscuits; or for dessert with whipped cream sweetened with a little maple syrup.

LIGHT CHOCOLATE SAUCE

2 tablespoons instant coffee	1 cup heavy cream
⅔ cup boiling water	1 tablespoon rum
1 cup semi-sweet chocolate	2 teaspoons vanilla
chips	1 extra-large egg

In bowl, dissolve instant coffee in boiling water.

In beaker, place chocolate chips; pour hot coffee into beaker. Blend on #6 speed for about 1 minute or until chips are melted. Add cream, rum, and vanilla; blend until combined. Add egg and blend again. Makes about 2½ cups.

Simply delicious drizzled over sliced bananas, angel food cake, ice cream, or fresh fruit. When refrigerated, it turns into chocolate pudding!

CHAPTER THREE

OMELETS AND EGG DISHES

MOSAIC OMELET WITH CHICKEN AND RED PEPPER
OMELET WITH CAMBOZOLA AND ASPARAGUS
RED PEPPER MUSHROOM OMELET
STRAWBERRY OMELET FOR LOVERS
OVEN OMELET WITH BOURSIN AND MUSHROOMS
RUM RAISIN FRENCH TOAST
CHEESE SOUFFLÉ
SCRAMBLED EGGS WITH GOAT CHEESE IN BRIOCHES
EGGS BENEDICT WITH ORANGE HOLLANDAISE
EGG FLORENTINE PIE

MOSAIC OMELET WITH CHICKEN AND RED PEPPER

¼ cup butter	1 cup cooked chicken,
10 Greek black olives	julienned
(Kalamata), pitted and	⅔ cup (about 3 ounces)
coarsely chopped	crumbled feta cheese
2 green onions, chopped	5 extra-large eggs
1 sweet red pepper, seeded	¼ cup light cream or milk
and diced	¼ teaspoon freshly ground
1 tablespoon capers, drained	black pepper

In heavy 10-inch non-stick skillet, melt 2 tablespoons butter over high heat. Add olives, green onions, red pepper, and capers. Cook for 4 minutes. Add chicken; cook until just heated through. Transfer mixture to a bowl; stir in feta cheese.

In same skillet, melt remaining butter over medium heat.

Meanwhile, in mixing bowl, blend eggs, cream, and pepper on #4 speed for 30 seconds. Pour egg mixture into skillet. As egg mixture begins to set, spoon chicken mixture over top of omelet.

Cover and reduce heat to low. Cook for 15 to 20 minutes or until omelet is set. Cut into 4 wedges. Serves 2 to 4.

OMELET WITH CAMBOZOLA AND ASPARAGUS

1 tablespoon butter	*2 ounces Cambozola cheese,*
3 extra-large eggs	*rind removed and cubed*
3 tablespoons milk	*6 spears fresh asparagus,*
¼ teaspoon freshly ground	*blanched and cut into*
black pepper	*½-inch pieces*

In 8-inch omelet pan or heavy skillet, melt butter over high heat.

In mixing bowl, blend eggs, milk, and pepper on #4 speed for 1 minute. Set aside.

When butter foams, but before it browns, pour in egg mixture. Stir gently with fork to expose egg to heat. When underside has set, lift edge of omelet using spatula and tilt pan so uncooked eggs flow underneath and set. When omelet begins to set, place Cambozola and asparagus in row across its center. Use fork to gently lift one third of omelet; fold it over center. Tilt pan and roll filled omelet over remaining third. Keep tilted over heat for 20 seconds to seal edges. Roll out onto warm serving plate. Serves 2.

Fabulous combination of blue cheese and asparagus. A very creamy, delightful spring omelet.

RED PEPPER MUSHROOM OMELET

4 extra-large eggs	1 tablespoon butter
2 tablespoons milk	2 large garlic cloves, minced
¼ teaspoon salt	½ large sweet red pepper,
¼ teaspoon freshly ground	seeded and cut into
black pepper	¼-inch strips
½ cup (about 2 ounces)	6 medium mushrooms, sliced
grated Jarlsberg,	Garnish:
mozzarella, or Cheddar	¼ cup fresh chopped parsley
cheese	

In mixing bowl, blend eggs, milk, salt, and pepper on #4 speed for 15 seconds. Stir in cheese. Set aside.

In medium, ovenproof skillet (cast iron omelet pan is perfect), melt butter over medium heat. Stir in garlic; cook 1 minute. Add egg mixture; cook for 3 to 5 minutes or until beginning to set. Top with red pepper and mushrooms. Place in preheated 350° oven; bake uncovered for 15 to 20 minutes or until omelet is set. Do not overcook. Remove from oven. Garnish with parsley and cut into wedges. Serves 2 to 4.

Attractive, puffy golden omelet, flecked with red pepper, mushrooms, and parsley.

STRAWBERRY OMELET FOR LOVERS

1 tablespoon butter	1 tablespoon strawberry jam
2 extra-large eggs	Garnish:
1 egg yolk	2 tablespoons sour cream
2 tablespoons milk	or plain yogurt
2 teaspoons sugar	2 whole strawberries
3 strawberries, chopped	

In heavy 8-inch omelet pan or skillet, melt butter over high heat.

Meanwhile, in mixing bowl, blend eggs, egg yolk, milk, and sugar on # 4 speed for 1 minute. Set aside.

When butter foams, but before it browns, pour in egg mixture. Stir gently with fork to expose egg to heat. When underside has set, lift edge of omelet using spatula and tilt pan so uncooked eggs flow underneath and set.

When omelet begins to set, place chopped strawberries and jam in row across center of omelet. Use fork to gently lift one third of omelet; fold it over center. Tilt pan and roll the filled portion over remaining one third of omelet. Keep tilted over heat for 20 seconds to seal edges. Roll out onto a warm serving plate and garnish with sour cream and strawberries. Serves 2.

A very sweet omelet for a romantic breakfast or brunch. Accompany with the driest of dry champagne.

OVEN OMELET WITH BOURSIN AND MUSHROOMS

3 extra-large eggs	*2 tablespoons butter*
¼ cup milk	*¾ cup sliced mushrooms*
1 tablespoon chopped fresh	*2 tablespoons Boursin cheese,*
basil or ½ teaspoon dried	*at room temperature*
Dash Tabasco	Garnish:
¼ teaspoon salt	*1 tomato, thinly sliced*
¼ teaspoon freshly ground	*¼ cup alfalfa sprouts*
black pepper	

In bowl, place eggs, milk, basil, Tabasco, salt, and pepper. Blend on #3 speed until combined. Set aside.

In medium non-stick skillet or omelet pan, melt 1 tablespoon butter over medium high heat. Cook mushrooms, stirring for 3 minutes or until brown. Add egg mixture and crumble in cheese. Place in preheated 350°F oven; bake for 20 minutes or until set.

Meanwhile, in small skillet over medium heat, melt remaining butter. Cook tomato slices for 2 minutes on each side or until warmed through. Cover and keep warm.

Remove omelet from oven, cut in half and garnish with warmed tomato and alfalfa sprouts. Serves 2.

RUM RAISIN FRENCH TOAST

3 eggs	½ teaspoon ground
1 egg yolk	cinnamon
1 cup milk	Pinch salt
2 tablespoons sugar	12 slices raisin bread
1 tablespoon light rum	¼ cup butter

In mixing bowl, blend eggs, egg yolk, milk, sugar, rum, cinnamon, and salt on #4 speed until combined. Place bread slices in shallow pan; pour egg mixture over. Soak for 10 minutes.

Meanwhile, in large skillet, melt butter over medium heat. Add bread slices and fry on both sides for 2 minutes or until golden brown. Transfer toast to baking sheet and keep warm in 150°F oven, while frying remaining bread. Makes 12 slices.

Delicious with maple syrup and sliced strawberries or spread Honey Pistachio Butter (see page 25) on top. Use whole-wheat raisin bread for slightly more nutrition. Like crêpes, cooked French toast can be successfully frozen between sheets of wax paper in plastic freezer containers and reheated on baking sheet in 300°F oven.

CHEESE SOUFFLÉ

2 tablespoons butter, melted	¼ cup (about 1 ounce)
¼ cup fine dry breadcrumbs	grated Gruyère cheese
¼ cup butter	¼ cup sour cream
¼ cup all-purpose floor	1 teaspoon Dijon mustard
¼ teaspoon salt	1 teaspoon Worcestershire sauce
1 cup milk	½ teaspoon dry mustard
1 cup (about 4 ounces) grated	⅛ teaspoon cayenne
Cheddar cheese	4 eggs, separated

Preheat oven to 375°F.

Prepare an 8-cup soufflé dish by brushing with melted butter and dusting with breadcrumbs.

In heavy medium saucepan, melt butter on low heat. Stir in flour and salt; cook 2 minutes. Do not brown butter. Slowly blend in milk on #3 speed until mixture thickens. Add Cheddar and Gruyère cheese, sour cream, mustard, Worcestershire sauce, dry mustard, and cayenne. Blend on #3 speed until cheese is melted and combined. Remove from heat and cool to room temperature. Add egg yolks; blend on #3 speed.

In mixing bowl, beat egg whites using whisk attachment on #2 speed until they are so stiff that you can turn bowl upside down without spilling them. Fold egg whites into cheese mixture and pour gently into soufflé dish. Bake 35 minutes. Serve immediately. Serves 4 to 6.

SCRAMBLED EGGS WITH GOAT CHEESE IN BRIOCHES

4 medium brioches	½ cup (about 2 ounces)
1 tablespoon butter	crumbled soft goat cheese
5 eggs	Garnish:
¼ cup light cream or milk	2 tablespoons sour cream
2 tablespoons chopped fresh	2 tablespoons salmon caviar
chives	(optional)
Pinch salt	2 tablespoons chopped chives
¼ teaspoon freshly ground	
black pepper	

Warm brioches in 300°F oven.

Meanwhile, in heavy medium skillet, melt butter over medium heat. In mixing bowl, blend eggs, cream, chives, salt, and pepper on #3 speed for 30 seconds; pour into skillet. Stir eggs with wooden spoon for about 2 minutes or until eggs begin to set. Sprinkle cheese on top of egg mixture. Scrambled eggs should be creamy, not dry.

Remove brioches from oven. Slice off tops; scoop out inside bread, leaving ½-inch shell. Fill with scrambled eggs; top with sour cream, caviar, if using, and chives. Place brioche lid on top of eggs. Serves 4.

Creamy scrambled eggs in brioches is an elegant-looking luncheon or brunch dish.

EGGS BENEDICT WITH ORANGE HOLLANDAISE

1 cup hot melted butter	*8 slices Canadian bacon*
3 egg yolks, at room	*2 teaspoons butter*
temperature	*1 orange, peeled and sliced*
Grated zest of 1 orange	*4 eggs*
1 tablespoon fresh lemon juice	*1 teaspoon white vinegar*
1 tablespoon fresh orange juice	Garnish:
Pinch cayenne	*Grated zest of 1 orange*
2 English muffins, split	

In small saucepan, heat butter until bubbly.

Meanwhile, in beaker, blend egg yolks, orange zest, lemon and orange juice, and cayenne on #6 speed until light and foamy. Pour hot melted butter into beaker in a steady stream while blending on #6 speed. Set aside.

Toast English muffins in a 200°F oven on baking sheet or in toaster, until golden. Butter and set aside on baking sheet.

In skillet, heat 1 teaspoon butter. Fry bacon until cooked, about 7 minutes; drain and place on top of muffins.

In same skillet, cook orange slices in remaining butter until warmed through. Place on top of bacon. Keep warm in oven.

Poach eggs in simmering water with 1 teaspoon vinegar. Transfer cooked eggs using slotted spoon to a paper-towel-lined plate. Dry well; place on muffin halves, on top of the orange slices.

Spoon orange hollandaise over poached eggs. Broil 1 minute or until golden brown. Garnish with orange zest. Serve immediately. Serves 2 to 4. Makes about 1¼ cups hollandaise sauce.

Very light, orange-flavored butter sauce. Try orange hollandaise with asparagus, or refrigerate sauce and use like a compound butter on grilled steak, fish, or baked potatoes. You can pre-poach eggs and store in bowl of ice water in refrigerator for up to 24 hours. To use, drain and reheat in saucepan of simmering water.

EGG FLORENTINE PIE

1 9-inch prepared deep-dish pie shell	½ cup (about 2 ounces) grated provolone cheese
2 tablespoons butter	1 tablespoon fresh basil or
5 ounces spinach, chopped	1 teaspoon dried
1 medium onion, chopped	½ teaspoon dried oregano
1 large garlic clove, minced	¼ teaspoon each nutmeg,
4 extra-large eggs	salt, and black pepper
½ cup light or heavy cream	6 slices tomato
1 cup (about 4 ounces) grated farmer's cheese or Havarti	2 tablespoons freshly grated Parmesan cheese

In 9-inch pie plate, bake pie shell in 400°F oven for 10 minutes. Set aside on cake rack.

In heavy skillet, melt 1 tablespoon butter over medium heat. Add spinach, onion, and garlic; cook, stirring, for 3 minutes or until spinach is wilted.

In mixing bowl, blend eggs, cream, farmer's and provolone cheeses, basil, oregano, nutmeg, salt, and pepper on #5 speed until combined. Add spinach mixture; blend on #5 speed until combined. Pour into cooled pie shell.

In skillet, melt remaining butter over medium-high heat. Cook tomatoes 1 minute, each side. Gently place on top of egg mixture in pie shell. Sprinkle with Parmesan cheese. Bake in 400°F oven for 30 to 35 minutes or until filling is set. Serves 4 to 6.

Red Pepper Mushroom Omelet (page 92) and Egg Florentine Pie (recipe this page)

BATTERS, PANCAKES, AND WAFFLES

*Clam Fritters (page 104) with
Lime Mayonnaise (page 60)*

CLAM FRITTERS

1 cup all-purpose flour	1 teaspoon vegetable oil
2 large eggs	¼ teaspoon salt
½ cup milk	3 dozen shucked littleneck
1 tablespoon fresh lemon	clams
juice	Oil for deep frying

In mixing bowl, blend flour, eggs, milk, lemon juice, oil, and salt on #3 speed until just combined. Stir in clams; refrigerate, covered, for 2 hours.

In deep fryer or wok, heat oil to 400°F. Using a teaspoon, drop one batter-covered clam into oil at a time, frying only as many clams as will fit without touching each other; cook for 5 minutes or until golden brown. Drain on paper-towel-lined plate. Repeat with remaining clams. Keep warm in a 400°F oven if necessary, but it is best to serve as they come out of the fryer. Salt them lightly and serve. Serves 4 to 6.

A favorite of New Englanders. Serve with Lime Mayonnaise (see page 60) or lemon wedges and lots of paper napkins.

BANANA FRITTERS

½ cup all-purpose flour	Oil for deep-frying
⅓ cup milk	2 to 3 bananas, cut into
1 egg	½-inch slices
1 tablespoon sugar	Icing sugar
2 teaspoons butter, melted	Ground cinnamon
Pinch salt	

In mixing bowl, blend flour, milk, egg, sugar, butter, and salt on #4 speed until combined. Refrigerate, covered, at least 1 hour.

In deep fryer or wok, heat oil to 400°F. Dip banana slices into batter; fry for about 5 minutes in batches until golden brown. Drain on paper-towel-lined plate. Sprinkle with icing sugar and cinnamon. Serve immediately. Makes about 25 fritters.

Hot bananas! Great idea for kids. Slice bananas just before dipping in batter.

CRÊPE BATTER

4 large eggs	¼ cup butter, melted
1½ cups milk	5 ice cubes
½ teaspoon salt	2 tablespoons vegetable oil
1 cup all-purpose flour	

In mixing bowl, using whisk attachment, whisk eggs, milk, and salt on #3 speed until combined. Gradually blend in flour. Whisk in melted butter. Stir in ice cubes and let batter stand at room temperature for 40 minutes or until cubes are melted. Blend again.

Lightly coat a heated 8-inch non-stick crêpe pan or heavy skillet with oil, using a paper towel.

Measure a scant ¼ cup batter and pour into prepared pan. Swirl batter around, lifting pan off medium high heat until skillet is thinly coated and batter begins to set. Cook for 1 minute, turn over and cook just until lightly browned, about 30 seconds. Remove to a plate and repeat process until batter is finished, brushing pan with oil in between cooking each crêpe if necessary. Makes 18 crêpes.

Beautiful, light crêpes which can be used immediately or prepared ahead. Use the crêpes for beggars' purses or add 2 tablespoons sugar to crêpe batter and fill with sweetened fruit. Spoon whipped cream over top and presto! Instant delectable dessert!

BLUEBERRY AND CHEESE BLINTZES

2½ cups fresh or thawed	3 cups (about 12 ounces)
frozen blueberries	grated farmer's cheese
¼ cup sugar	2 tablespoons butter
Grated zest of 1 orange	Sugar
1 tablespoon fresh orange juice	Ground cinnamon
1 tablespoon fresh lemon juice	1½ cups sour cream or plain
12 prepared crêpes	yogurt
(see page 106)	

To make blueberry sauce, in heavy saucepan cook blueberries, sugar, orange zest, orange juice, and lemon juice over medium heat, stirring, until thick and syrupy, about 5 minutes. Set aside.

In center of each crêpe, place a heaping tablespoon of grated farmer's cheese; top with 1 tablespoon blueberry sauce. Fold edges of crêpes envelope style, to make a square.

In large heavy skillet, melt butter over medium heat. Place crêpes seam side down and fry for 2 minutes on each side or until golden. Transfer to warm plates; sprinkle crêpes with sugar and cinnamon. Serve with dollop of sour cream or yogurt. Makes 12 crêpes.

Terrific for a special breakfast or to feed a hungry crowd at brunch. They may be made a few hours ahead before frying, covered well, and refrigerated.

107

CRÊPES WITH CHICKEN MUSHROOM FILLING

¼ cup butter	¼ teaspoon freshly ground
4 cups sliced (about 10	black pepper
ounces) fresh mushrooms	1 cup (about 4 ounces) grated
8 green onions, chopped	Emmentaler cheese
¼ cup all-purpose flour	4 cups cooked chicken
2 cups chicken stock	(2 pounds boneless chicken
½ cup dry white vermouth	breasts), cubed
1 tablespoon Dijon mustard	20 prepared crêpes
2 teaspoons dried tarragon	(see page 106)
¼ teaspoon salt	

In heavy saucepan, melt butter over medium heat. Add mushrooms and green onions; cook 5 minutes or until golden. Remove to bowl using slotted spoon; set aside. Add flour to saucepan and stir, using wooden spoon, until golden. Add stock, vermouth, mustard, tarragon, salt, and pepper and blend on #3 speed until thickened. Add ½ cup cheese; blend until cheese is melted. Reserve ½ cup sauce. Set aside.

Return mushroom-green-onion mixture to saucepan. Stir in chicken. Place about ¼ cup chicken mixture at outer edge of crêpes; roll up gently and tuck in ends. Place in greased 9 x 13-inch baking dish. Spoon remaining sauce over crêpes. Sprinkle remaining cheese on top and bake in preheated 400°F oven for 15 to 20 minutes or until bubbling. Makes 20 crêpes.

SPOON BREAD

Butter	3 eggs, separated
2 cups milk	2 tablespoons butter
½ cup yellow cornmeal	½ teaspoon salt

Lightly grease a 6-cup baking or soufflé dish.

In heavy medium saucepan, bring milk to a boil. Slowly blend in cornmeal on #4 speed. Remove saucepan from heat; let stand 5 minutes. Blend in egg yolks, 2 tablespoons butter, and salt on #6 speed.

In beaker, beat egg whites on #2 speed, using whisk attachment, until soft peaks form.

In saucepan, fold egg whites into cornmeal mixture using a spatula. Pour cornmeal mixture into prepared baking dish. Bake in 350°F oven for 30 minutes or until golden brown. Serve immediately. Serves 4 to 6.

A Southern side dish usually served with ham and chicken. The center should be slightly moist, as it cooks between standing and serving time. It should not be completely dry. For additional flavor, sprinkle some grated Parmesan cheese on the buttered soufflé dish and some on top of the mixture. Chopped fresh parsley can also be added to the mixture.

WAFFLES

4 extra-large eggs, separated	1 cup whole-wheat flour
1 cup butter, melted	1 cup all-purpose flour
1½ cups buttermilk	2½ teaspoons baking powder
1 cup sour cream or plain	¾ teaspoon baking soda
yogurt	½ teaspoon salt
2 tablespoons sugar	Butter

In mixing bowl, blend egg yolks, melted butter, buttermilk, sour cream, and sugar on #6 speed.

In separate bowl, combine whole-wheat flour, all-purpose flour, baking powder, baking soda, and salt. Add to egg mixture and blend until combined. Set aside.

In beaker, using whisk attachment, beat egg whites on #2 speed until fluffy, and soft peaks form. Fold into batter.

Butter waffle iron well and heat. Pour ⅓ cup batter into waffle iron, close cover, and cook until golden brown, about 2 minutes. Cook remaining waffles in the same manner. Makes about 20 4-inch square waffles.

Serve with Apple Butter (see page 35), maple syrup, or homemade conserves. Create your own waffle sandwich by layering softened vanilla ice cream in between two waffles and sprinkling icing sugar on top. Serve with fresh strawberries.

PANCAKES

¾ cup all-purpose flour	½ cup milk
1 teaspoon sugar	2 tablespoons butter, melted
1 teaspoon baking powder	1 extra-large egg
¼ teaspoon salt	Vegetable oil

In mixing bowl, combine flour, sugar, baking powder, and salt. Add milk, butter, and egg; blend on #6 speed until just combined. Do not overmix.

In large skillet heat oil over medium heat. Pour ¼ cup batter into heated skillet. Cook for 2 minutes or until bubbles appear on surface; flip over and cook for 1 minute or until golden brown. Cook remaining pancakes in the same manner and add more oil to pan if necessary to prevent sticking. Makes 6 pancakes.

Serve these light pancakes with orange butter (softened butter blended on #3 speed with orange zest and a little juice) or maple syrup.

OATMEAL PANCAKES

1 cup quick-cooking oatmeal	¼ teaspoon baking soda
(not instant)	⅛ teaspoon salt
1¼ cups buttermilk	⅓ cup butter, melted
½ cup all-purpose flour	1 extra-large egg
½ teaspoon baking powder	Butter or oil

In medium bowl, mix together oatmeal and buttermilk; soak 30 minutes.

In mixing bowl, combine flour, baking powder, baking soda, and salt. Add soaked oatmeal mixture, butter and egg. Blend on #5 speed until just combined.

Heat butter or oil in heavy skillet or griddle over medium heat. Pour ¼ cup batter into heated skillet — enough to make each pancake a 3-inch round. Cook for 2 minutes or until several bubbles appear on surface, flip over and cook for 2 minutes more, or until golden brown. Serve immediately. Makes 10 pancakes.

Delicious with Honey Pistachio Butter (see page 25), Red Wine and Apricot Butter (see page 26) or Apple Butter (see page 35).

POPOVERS

3 eggs	¼ teaspoon salt
1 cup milk	⅓ cup (approximately)
1 cup all-purpose flour	vegetable oil

Preheat oven to 450°F.

In medium bowl, blend eggs, milk, flour, and salt on #6 speed until well combined. Let batter stand at room temperature for 30 minutes.

Place about 2 teaspoons vegetable oil into each of 12 medium-size muffin cups. Place muffin pan in oven for 3 to 5 minutes or until oil is hot. Watch carefully. Remove pan from oven and fill cups ⅔ full. Place muffin pan on cookie sheet with sides, to catch any spillover, and place in oven on middle rack for 20 to 30 minutes or until puffed and browned. Serve at once.

Do not open oven door while baking or popovers might not puff up! As a variation, add 1 teaspoon dried herbs, such as thyme, sage, or basil to batter. For sweet popovers add 1/4 cup sugar to batter; serve with orange butter (see page 111).

CHAPTER FIVE

SOUPS

SPINACH SOUP

¼ cup butter	½ teaspoon freshly ground
1½ cups finely chopped onion	black pepper
(about 1 large)	1 (10-ounce/284-g) package
2 leeks, cleaned and thinly	of fresh spinach, finely
sliced	chopped
3 large garlic cloves, minced	½ cup plain yogurt
4 cups chicken stock	Juice of ½ lemon
½ pound potatoes (about 3	Dash Tabasco
small), peeled and diced	Garnish:
¼ teaspoon freshly grated	⅓ cup sour cream or
nutmeg	plain yogurt
½ teaspoon salt	Grated zest of 1 lemon

In large heavy saucepan, melt butter over medium-high heat. Stir in onions, leeks, and garlic; cook, stirring occasionally, for 5 minutes or until soft. Add stock, potatoes, nutmeg, salt, and pepper; simmer, uncovered, over medium-low heat for 20 minutes or until potatoes are tender. Add spinach; simmer for 15 minutes.

In saucepan, blend on #6 speed until combined. Stir in yogurt, lemon juice and Tabasco to taste. Garnish with dollop of sour cream or yogurt and sprinkle lemon zest on top. Serves 7.

CARROT AND TOMATO SOUP

¼ cup butter	1 teaspoon dried thyme
3 medium tomatoes, peeled, seeded, and chopped	1 teaspoon Worcestershire sauce
½ pound carrots, peeled and thinly sliced	½ teaspoon salt
½ pound potatoes (about 3 small), peeled and diced	½ teaspoon freshly ground black pepper
1 cup finely chopped onion (about 1 medium)	Garnish: 2 tomatoes, chopped
3 cups chicken stock	2 carrots, julienned
½ cup dry red wine	½ cup sour cream or plain yogurt

In large saucepan, melt butter over medium-high heat. Add tomatoes, carrots, potatoes, and onion, stirring occasionally, for about 5 minutes or until onions are soft. Add chicken stock, red wine, thyme, Worcestershire sauce, salt, and pepper. Simmer over medium-low heat for 30 minutes or until vegetables are soft. Blend on #6 speed until smooth, but with some texture. Heat through and garnish with chopped tomato, carrot, and a dollop of sour cream or yogurt. Serves 4 to 6.

This pretty, light-orange-colored soup has great flavor and an interesting texture.

WATERCRESS SOUP

¼ cup butter	3 cups chicken stock
6 green onions, finely chopped	½ teaspoon dried summer
1 cup finely chopped onion	savory
(about 1 medium)	¼ teaspoon salt
½ pound potatoes (about 1	¼ teaspoon freshly ground
large), peeled and diced	black pepper
3 bunches watercress, finely	¾ cup heavy or light cream
chopped	

In large heavy saucepan or Dutch oven, melt butter over medium-high heat. Add green onions, onion, and potatoes; cook, stirring, for 4 to 5 minutes. Stir in watercress; cook, stirring, for 4 minutes. Add chicken stock, savory, salt, and pepper. Bring to a boil; reduce heat to medium-low and simmer, uncovered, for about 30 minutes or until potatoes are soft. Blend on #6 speed until combined and puréed. Add cream; blend again. Heat through gently. Serves 6.

Also delicious served cold.

TOMATO AND CRAB BISQUE

1 tablespoon butter	¼ teaspoon Tabasco
½ cup chopped onion	¼ teaspoon freshly ground
½ cup finely chopped celery	black pepper
3 mushrooms, chopped	Garnish:
3 cups Easy Cream of Tomato	2 tablespoons chopped fresh
Soup (see page 122)	dill
⅓ cup port	1 medium tomato, peeled,
1 can (4.5 ounce/128-g)	seeded, and chopped
crabmeat, drained	

In large heavy saucepan, melt butter over medium heat. Add onion, celery, and mushrooms; cook, stirring occasionally, for about 5 minutes or until soft.

Add Easy Cream of Tomato Soup and port; simmer over medium-low heat for 10 minutes. Blend on #6 speed until smooth.

Chop crabmeat coarsely; stir into soup. Add Tabasco and pepper. Garnish with fresh dill and tomato. Serves 4.

A very creamy and textured soup that looks lovely with its garnish of green dill and red tomato. Serve with crusty French bread and a green salad.

AVOCADO BISQUE

2 tablespoons vegetable oil	6 drops Tabasco, or to taste
¾ cup chopped onion	¼ teaspoon salt
(about 1 large)	¼ teaspoon freshly ground
4 cups chicken stock	black pepper
2 teaspoons dried tarragon	5 small ripe avocados
or 1 tablespoon fresh	(about 2 pounds), peeled
1 tablespoon fresh lemon	and chopped
juice	2 cups milk or light cream
2 teaspoons tarragon vinegar	

In heavy medium saucepan, heat oil over medium high heat. Add onion; cook for 4 minutes or until soft. Add stock, tarragon, lemon juice, tarragon vinegar, Tabasco, salt, and pepper. Bring to a boil. Add avocados. Reduce heat and simmer for 15 minutes. Remove from heat. Add milk. Blend mixture on #5 speed until smooth. Serve hot or cold. Serves 6.

This velvety, pale green, and very rich soup is for avocado lovers.

BROCCOLI SOUP

½ cup butter	1½ teaspoons celery seed
1 large bunch broccoli	½ teaspoon salt
(about 1 pound), chopped	½ teaspoon freshly ground
(include stems; save some	black pepper
florets for garnish)	5 cups chicken stock
1 cup finely chopped parsley	Garnish:
¾ cup finely chopped celery	Blanched broccoli florets
1½ teaspoons dried marjoram	

In large heavy saucepan or Dutch oven, melt butter over medium heat. Add broccoli, parsley, and celery; cook, stirring, uncovered, for about 7 minutes or until tender. Stir in marjoram, celery seed, salt, pepper, and stock. Simmer over medium-low heat for about 15 minutes or until vegetables are soft.

Meanwhile, blanch remaining broccoli florets in boiling water in small saucepan. Drain; refresh under cold water. Set aside.

Remove saucepan from heat and blend soup on #6 speed until desired consistency is reached. Adjust seasoning if necessary. Garnish with broccoli florets before serving. Serves 6.

Bursts of broccoli flavor fill this refreshing, gorgeous green soup. For an enriched soup, add 1/2 cup light or heavy cream — but taste it first without! Serve for lunch with crusty Italian rolls and a wedge of Brie.

EASY CREAM OF TOMATO SOUP

2 cans (each 28-ounce/	2 cups heavy cream
796-mL) tomatoes,	¾ teaspoon salt
undrained	¾ teaspoon freshly ground
2 cups milk	black pepper

In heavy noncorrosive saucepan, blend tomatoes and liquid on #6 speed until smooth. Add milk, cream, salt, and pepper; blend again. Cook gently over medium heat and serve. Serves 10.

Very tomatoey in taste. I like to add fresh chopped herbs such as basil, oregano, chervil, or marjoram as a variation. Or toss in heart-shaped garlic toasts and sprinkle chopped fresh basil on top for a romantic starter to dinner.

LEEK, ONION, AND POTATO SOUP

¼ cup butter	1 stalk celery, finely chopped
¾ pound potatoes (about 2 medium), peeled and diced	4 cups chicken stock
	1 cup heavy or light cream
3 cups leeks (about 4-5 medium) cleaned and chopped (include some of the green)	2 tablespoons fresh lemon juice
	½ teaspoon salt
	½ teaspoon freshly ground black pepper
2½ cups green onions, finely chopped (white part only)	

In large heavy saucepan, melt butter over medium heat. Add potatoes, leeks, green onions, and celery. Cook, stirring occasionally, for 5 minutes or until soft but not browned.

Add chicken stock. Simmer uncovered for 20 minutes or until vegetables are soft. In saucepan, blend on #6 speed until smooth. Stir in cream, lemon juice, salt, and pepper. Heat gently over low heat, stirring. Serves 7.

A pale green soup with lots of leek flavor. Lemon juice gives it a fresh tangy taste. Float croutons on top with a dollop of sour cream or yogurt swirled in. Serve with scones or drop biscuits.

CELERY SOUP

¼ cup butter	¼ teaspoon salt
6 stalks celery, trimmed and minced	¼ teaspoon freshly ground black pepper
2 cups finely chopped onion (about 2 medium)	½ cup mashed potatoes (see page 166)
5 green onions, finely chopped	½ cup sour cream
	2 tablespoons milk
¼ cup chopped fresh parsley	Garnish:
4 cups chicken stock	Fresh parsley, chopped

In large heavy saucepan, melt butter over medium heat. Add celery, onions, green onions, and parsley; cook for 5 minutes. Stir in chicken stock, salt, and pepper; simmer over medium-low heat for about 30 minutes or until vegetables are very soft.

In beaker, place mashed potatoes with 1 cup of soup and blend on #3 speed until combined. Return mixture to saucepan and blend soup on #3 speed until it reaches desired consistency. Stir in sour cream and milk. Heat gently over low heat. Do not boil or sour cream may curdle. Garnish with chopped parsley. Serves 6.

Excellent, pure celery flavor. Very tasty served for lunch accompanied by a whole-grain bread.

SQUASH AND APPLE SOUP

¼ cup butter	6 cups chicken stock
3 Granny Smith apples,	2 tablespoons cider vinegar
peeled, cored, and cubed	¾ teaspoon salt
1 small onion, thinly sliced	¾ teaspoon freshly ground
1 pound butternut squash,	black pepper
peeled, seeded, and cubed	

In large heavy saucepan, melt butter over medium heat. Add apples, onion, and squash; cook for 5 minutes, stirring occasionally. Add chicken stock and vinegar. Bring to a boil; simmer, uncovered, for about 30 minutes or until vegetables are soft. Add salt and pepper. In saucepan, blend on #6 speed until puréed. Adjust seasoning if necessary and serve. Serves 6.

No cream is needed in this golden smooth soup. It has lots of body without adding extra calories and fat. Garnish with a dollop of yogurt or sour cream or swirl it in, leaving a streaky effect.

CREAM OF ARTICHOKE SOUP

½ cup butter	*4 cups chicken stock*
1 leek, cleaned and finely	*¼ teaspoon salt*
chopped (white part only)	*¼ teaspoon freshly ground*
2 cans (each 14-ounce/	*black pepper*
398-mL) artichoke hearts,	*1 cup heavy cream*
drained and chopped	Garnish:
½ cup finely chopped parsley	*Freshly chopped chives*

In large heavy saucepan, melt butter over medium heat. Add leeks and cook for about 5 minutes or until soft. Add artichokes and parsley; cook for 2 minutes. Stir in stock and simmer, uncovered, for 15 minutes. Add salt and pepper and blend on #6 speed until smooth. Add cream, and reheat gently. Garnish with chopped chives. Serves 7.

A rich soup with a very pronounced artichoke flavor.

GAZPACHO

1 can (19-ounce/540-mL) tomato juice	1 tablespoon chopped fresh parsley
1/3 cup olive oil	1 tablespoon chopped fresh
1/3 cup red wine vinegar	dill or 1 teaspoon dried
2 cups coarsely chopped tomatoes	1 tablespoon chopped fresh basil or 1 teaspoon dried
1 sweet red pepper, seeded and diced	2 teaspoons Worcestershire sauce
1 sweet green pepper, seeded and diced	1/2 teaspoon Tabasco Salt
1 sweet yellow pepper, seeded and diced	Freshly ground black pepper Garnish:
1 large onion, finely chopped	Chopped fresh parsley or chives Croutons

In large mixing bowl, blend tomato juice, olive oil, vinegar, tomatoes, sweet peppers, onion, parsley, dill, basil, Worcestershire sauce, Tabasco, salt, and pepper to taste on #6 speed until combined. The soup will not be smooth but will retain some texture. Chill several hours before serving. Taste and correct seasoning if necessary. Sprinkle with parsley and croutons. Serves 6 to 8.

A cooling summer soup and very flavorful.

CREAM OF GREEN PEA SOUP

¼ cup butter	1 tablespoon dried tarragon
1½ cups chopped onion	or 2 tablespoons chopped
(about 1 large)	fresh
½ head iceberg lettuce,	1 tablespoon dried mint or
finely shredded	2 tablespoons chopped fresh
¼ cup chopped fresh parsley	¾ teaspoon salt
2 pound (1-kg) package	¾ teaspoon freshly ground
frozen peas	black pepper
4 cups chicken stock	1 cup light cream
1 tablespoon dried chervil or	Garnish:
3 tablespoons chopped fresh	Fresh mint leaves

In large heavy saucepan, melt butter over medium heat. Add onion and cook for 5 minutes or until soft. Stir in lettuce and parsley; cook for 2 minutes. Add 6 cups peas, stock, chervil, tarragon, mint, salt, and pepper. Simmer, uncovered, over medium-low heat for 10 minutes or until vegetables are soft. In saucepan, blend on #6 speed until smooth. Stir in cream; cook gently over low heat, until heated through. Garnish with remaining thawed peas and mint leaves. Serves 8 to 10.

Yummy pea flavor. This soup has an interesting texture if you do not sieve it.

PEACH YOGURT SOUP

1 can (28-ounce/796-mL) peach halves in light syrup	1 tablespoon chopped fresh mint or 1 teaspoon dried
Finely grated zest of 2 oranges	⅛ teaspoon freshly grated nutmeg
1 cup fresh orange juice (about 2 large oranges)	1 cinnamon stick
¼ cup pale dry sherry	1⅓ cups plain yogurt
¼ cup sugar	Garnish:
	Fresh mint leaves

Strain peach syrup into medium saucepan.

In beaker, blend peaches on #6 speed until smooth. Place peaches, orange zest, orange juice, sherry, sugar, mint, nutmeg, and cinnamon stick in saucepan with peach syrup. Blend on #3 speed over medium-low heat for 1 minute, or until sugar dissolves. Remove from heat. Let cool to room temperature. Stir in yogurt. Chill overnight. Remove cinnamon stick, garnish with fresh mint leaves, and serve. Serves 6.

A cool refreshing soup that tastes like fresh peaches! Serve well chilled before or after main course. Add a dollop of yogurt swirled through the top for a pretty effect.

RED LENTIL SOUP

3 tablespoons butter	4 cups chicken stock
1 tablespoon olive oil	3 tablespoons fresh lemon
2 cups cleaned, chopped	juice
leeks (about 3 medium),	¼ teaspoon salt
white part only	¼ teaspoon freshly ground
1 cup chopped onion	black pepper
(about 1 medium)	6 ounces ham, diced
1 cup red lentils	

In large heavy saucepan or Dutch oven, heat butter and oil over medium heat. Stir in leeks, onion, and lentils; cook for 5 minutes or until soft. Add chicken stock, lemon juice, salt, and pepper. Bring to boil; reduce heat and simmer, covered, for 20 to 30 minutes or until lentils are tender. In saucepan, blend on #4 speed until smooth. Stir in ham; simmer, covered, for 15 minutes longer. Serves 4 to 6.

A savory, thick, heartwarming soup.

RASPBERRY SOUP WITH ORANGE

1 cup sugar	*1 cup fresh orange juice*
1 cup water	*(about 2 large oranges)*
Finely grated zest of 2 oranges	*2 cups heavy cream*
2 packages (each 12-ounce/	Garnish:
300-g) frozen unsweetened	*1 pint fresh raspberries*
raspberries	*Mint sprigs*

In heavy medium saucepan, place sugar, water, and orange zest. Cook, stirring gently, over high heat until boiling. Cook, uncovered (do not stir) for 15 minutes or until slightly thickened. Set aside.

In separate saucepan, cook raspberries with orange juice over medium-high heat for 10 minutes, or until berries are no longer frozen. Blend on #4 speed until puréed. Strain through a sieve into sugar syrup. Blend on #3 speed, adding cream while blending. Chill. Garnish with fresh raspberries and mint sprigs. Serves 4 to 6.

A sweet dessert soup with a fresh and creamy taste.

CHEDDAR CHEESE SOUP

¼ cup butter	2 tablespoons all-purpose flour
1⅔ cups chopped red onion (about 1 large)	4 cups chicken stock
	½ cup dry white vermouth
2 large garlic cloves, minced	½ cup heavy or light cream
½ teaspoon freshly ground black pepper	4 cups (about 1 pound) grated Cheddar cheese

In large heavy saucepan, melt butter over medium-high heat. Add onion, garlic, and pepper; cook for about 5 minutes or until soft. Add flour and cook, stirring constantly, with a wooden spoon, until flour begins to turn a golden color. Remove saucepan from heat and add stock and vermouth. Blend in saucepan on #6 speed and return to heat. Bring to a boil. Reduce heat to low and stir in cream and cheese; simmer very gently until cheese melts and blend again. *Do not boil* once the cheese has been added. Serves 6.

Delicious flavor — a star soup! It is a pretty light orange color with purple flecks from the red onion. Garlic toasts floating in this soup would be an asset or garnish with saffron threads.

CHAPTER SIX

MAIN COURSES

SPAGHETTI WITH CARBONARA SAUCE
SPAGHETTI OR MACARONI WITH CHEDDAR SCALLION SAUCE
PENNE OR RIGATONI WITH TOMATO AND HOT SAUSAGE SAUCE
LINGUINE WITH TOMATO CLAM SAUCE
MANICOTTI
MEXICAN CHICKEN
TANDOORI CHICKEN
CHICKEN CURRY WITH FRESH BASIL
TURKEY TONNATO
PORK TENDERLOIN IN RED CURRANT AND WINE SAUCE
SPARERIBS WITH APPLE CINNAMON GLAZE
MARINATED BUTTERFLIED LEG OF LAMB
GRILLED LAMB CHOPS WITH MUSTARD HERB GARLIC BUTTER
STEAK WITH WINE SAUCE
HALIBUT STEAK WITH JULIENNE OF CARROT AND LEEK SAUCE
GRILLED SWORDFISH KEBABS WITH WASABI-HERB BUTTER
SHRIMP IN SAFFRON SAUCE
SALMON WITH SORREL SPINACH SAUCE
WELSH RAREBIT
QUICHE LORRAINE

SPAGHETTI WITH CARBONARA SAUCE

2 large eggs	¾ pound bacon, cut into
⅓ cup heavy cream	½-inch pieces
¼ teaspoon freshly grated	2 large garlic cloves, minced
nutmeg	1 medium tomato, chopped
¼ teaspoon salt	¾ pound spaghetti
¼ teaspoon freshly ground	¼ cup freshly grated
black pepper	Parmesan cheese

In bowl, blend eggs, cream, nutmeg, salt, and pepper on #4 speed until combined. Pour into wide serving bowl. Set aside.

In small skillet, cook bacon until crisp. Transfer to paper-towel-lined plate to drain, reserving 1 teaspoon bacon fat.

In same skillet with reserved bacon fat, cook garlic over medium heat for 1 minute. Add tomato; cook for 5 minutes or until soft. Set aside.

In plenty of boiling salted water, cook spaghetti until *al dente* (tender but firm). Drain and place on top of egg mixture. Toss with 2 forks until well coated with sauce. Add cooked tomato; toss. Garnish with cooked bacon and Parmesan cheese. Serves 4 to 6.

Carbonara sauce with a difference! The tomato isn't traditional, but it adds lovely color and flavor. Pass the pepper mill and extra grated Parmesan cheese at the table.

Spaghetti with Carbonara Sauce
(recipe this page)

SPAGHETTI OR MACARONI WITH CHEDDAR SCALLION SAUCE

1 tablespoon butter	1 tablespoon Dijon mustard
1 tablespoon flour	2 cups (about 8 ounces)
1 cup milk, scalded	grated Cheddar cheese
¼ teaspoon salt	4 green onions, finely chopped
¼ teaspoon freshly ground	¾ pound spaghetti or
black pepper	macaroni
⅛ teaspoon freshly grated	
nutmeg	

In medium saucepan, melt butter over medium heat. Remove saucepan from heat; add flour and stir, using wooden spoon. Return to heat; slowly add milk, stirring constantly. Add salt, pepper, and nutmeg; cook for 5 minutes or until thickened.

Remove saucepan from heat; add mustard and cheese; blend on #3 speed until cheese melts. Stir in green onions.

Meanwhile, in plenty of salted water, cook spaghetti or macaroni until *al dente* (tender but firm). Drain and toss with sauce. Serves 2 to 4.

A wonderful, creamy sauce that is quick and delicious. Try it over fettuccine, too.

Hot 'n' Spicy Peanut Sauce (page 85) with grilled chicken and pork

PENNE OR RIGATONI WITH TOMATO AND HOT SAUSAGE SAUCE

2 tablespoons olive oil	1 tablespoon fresh chopped dill
1 hot Italian sausage (about	1 teaspoon dried basil
½ pound), casing removed	¼ teaspoon fennel seeds
1 medium onion, chopped	¼ teaspoon salt
2 large garlic cloves, minced	¼ teaspoon freshly ground
2 tablespoons chopped fresh	black pepper
parsley	½ pound penne or rigatoni
1½ pounds ripe tomatoes	Freshly grated Parmesan
(about 4 medium), chopped	cheese

In heavy saucepan, heat olive oil over medium-high heat and crumble sausage into pan. Cook, breaking up lumps with fork, for 5 minutes or until lightly browned. Remove sausage from pan. Set aside.

Add onion, garlic, and parsley to pan; cook for 4 minutes or until onion is soft. Add tomatoes and blend on #6 speed until combined. Add cooked sausage, dill, basil, fennel seeds, salt, and pepper; simmer for 15 minutes or until slightly thickened. Keep warm.

In plenty of boiling salted water, cook pasta until *al dente* (tender but firm). Drain. Toss pasta with sauce and serve immediately. Pass the pepper mill and grated Parmesan cheese at the table. Serves 2 to 4. Makes about 3 cups sauce.

LINGUINE WITH TOMATO CLAM SAUCE

2 tablespoons olive oil	¼ teaspoon salt
1 tablespoon butter	¼ teaspoon freshly ground
2 medium onions, chopped	black pepper
3 large garlic cloves, chopped	1 can (5-ounce/142-g) baby
1 can (28-ounce/796-mL)	clams, drained
tomatoes, undrained	1 pound linguine
½ cup dry white vermouth	Garnish:
¼ cup chopped fresh parsley	2 tablespoons chopped fresh
3 tablespoons fresh basil or	parsley
1 tablespoon dried	¼ cup freshly grated
1 teaspoon dry mustard	Parmesan cheese
½ teaspoon ground	
cinnamon	

In medium noncorrosive saucepan, heat olive oil and butter over medium heat. Add onion and garlic; cook for 5 minutes or until soft. Add tomatoes, vermouth, parsley, basil, dry mustard, cinnamon, salt, and pepper. Simmer for 30 minutes or until slightly thickened. Remove saucepan from heat. Blend on #6 speed until tomatoes are puréed (onions won't be). Return saucepan to medium heat. Stir in clams. Taste and adjust seasonings if necessary.

Meanwhile, in plenty of boiling salted water, cook linguine until *al dente* (tender but firm) and drain. Pour sauce over pasta and toss well. Garnish with parsley and Parmesan cheese. Serves 5. Makes about 3¾ cups sauce.

MANICOTTI

Sauce:	1½ cups (about 6 ounces)
1 tablespoon butter	grated mozzarella cheese
2 tablespoons olive oil	½ cup freshly grated
1 medium onion, chopped	Parmesan cheese
1 can (28-ounce/796-mL)	¼ cup freshly grated
tomatoes, undrained	Romano cheese
¼ teaspoon salt	Béchamel Sauce:
½ teaspoon freshly ground	3 tablespoons butter
black pepper	3 tablespoons all-purpose flour
1 tablespoon chopped fresh	2 cups warm milk
basil or 1 teaspoon dried	Pinch each, salt, white pepper,
1 teaspoon dried oregano	and nutmeg
1½ cups chicken stock	½ cup freshly grated
Filling:	Parmesan cheese
1 package (10 ounces)	
spinach, finely chopped	1 package (250-g) manicotti
1 pound (about 2 cups)	noodles
ricotta cheese	¼ cup freshly grated
2 eggs	Parmesan cheese
¼ teaspoon each salt, pepper,	
and nutmeg	

To make sauce: in heavy saucepan, heat butter and oil over medium heat.

Add onion and cook for 3 minutes or until soft. Stir in tomatoes, salt, pepper, basil, oregano, and chicken stock; blend on #4 speed until coarsely puréed. Simmer, uncovered, over medium-low heat for 30 minutes or until thickened. Blend again if smoother consistency is desired.

To make filling: in large mixing bowl, blend spinach, ricotta, eggs, salt, pepper, and nutmeg on #6 speed until combined. Add mozzarella, Parmesan, and Romano cheeses; stir, using wooden spoon, until well mixed. Set aside.

To make béchamel sauce: in heavy saucepan, melt butter over medium heat. Add flour; cook, stirring with wooden spoon for 3 minutes. Do not let flour brown. Remove saucepan from heat. Slowly add milk, blending on #3 speed. Scrape down sides of pan with spatula if necessary. Return to heat. As sauce begins to thicken add salt, pepper, and nutmeg. Remove from heat; add Parmesan cheese and continue blending until thickened. Cover with piece of buttered wax paper and keep warm.

To assemble manicotti: cook noodles in boiling salted water until *al dente* (tender but firm). Drain; place in bowl of cold water. Drain and dry using paper toweling. Stuff manicotti with filling.

In 9 x 13-inch baking pan, spoon half the tomato sauce over bottom of pan. Place stuffed manicotti on top of sauce; cover with remainder of tomato sauce. Spoon béchamel down the center of baking pan. Sprinkle with Parmesan cheese and bake in 350°F oven for 35 minutes or until bubbly. Makes about 16 manicotti.

Much easier to prepare than it looks. It's hearty and delicious. Serve with a crisp green salad tossed with Creamy Garlic Dressing (see page 75).

MEXICAN CHICKEN

2 tablespoons olive oil	½ teaspoon chili powder,
¼ cup finely chopped red	or to taste
onion	4 chicken breasts (about
2 large garlic cloves, minced	2 pounds)
3 pickled jalapeño peppers,	2 cups (about 8 ounces)
chopped	grated Monterey Jack or
1 large tomato, chopped	Cheddar cheese
1 tablespoon chopped fresh	Garnish:
parsley	8 green onions, chopped
2 tablespoons fresh lemon	2 large tomatoes, chopped
juice	1 package (7-ounce/200-g)
1 can (14-ounce/398-mL)	tortilla chips
refried beans	1 cup sour cream

In medium saucepan, heat oil over medium-high heat. Add onion, garlic, peppers, tomato, parsley, and lemon juice; cook, stirring, for 3 minutes. Add refried beans and chili powder to taste; blend in saucepan on #6 speed for 30 seconds or until combined. Reduce heat to medium; cook, stirring, for 4 minutes. Set aside.

Place chicken in small roasting pan. Bake in 400°F oven for 35 to 40 minutes or until chicken is no longer pink.

While chicken is still warm, remove meat from bone. Hand pull chicken into thick strips; place on heatproof platter. Top with warm bean dip. Sprinkle cheese on top. Place platter under broiler for 1 or 2 minutes or until chicken is reheated and cheese melts; remove and garnish with green onions and tomatoes. Place tortilla chips around edge of platter. Pass sour cream at the table. Serves 4 to 6.

A hearty, piquant taste of Mexico. Very satisfying with a glass of cold beer. Chopped fresh coriander would be a delicious addition to the garnish. This bean dip can also be used as a warm dip with tortilla chips and slices of jícama.

TANDOORI CHICKEN

1 cup plain yogurt	1 teaspoon salt
¼ cup fresh lime juice	½ teaspoon ground cumin
(about 2 limes)	½ teaspoon dry mustard
2 tablespoons vegetable oil	½ teaspoon cayenne
4 large garlic cloves, chopped	½ teaspoon freshly ground
2 tablespoons minced fresh	black pepper
ginger	¼ teaspoon turmeric
1 teaspoon curry powder	4 chicken breasts

In beaker, blend yogurt, lime juice, oil, garlic, ginger, curry powder, salt, cumin, mustard, cayenne, pepper, and turmeric on #5 speed until combined.

In shallow baking pan, pour marinade over chicken breasts. Refrigerate several hours or overnight, turning occasionally.

Grill or broil chicken breasts, basting with marinade until golden brown, about 10 minutes per side, or until no longer pink at the bone. Serves 2 to 4.

The combination of yogurt, lime juice, and seasonings in this marinade creates extremely succulent grilled chicken. I also like to use this marinade with chicken wings.

CHICKEN CURRY WITH FRESH BASIL

¼ cup all-purpose flour	2 teaspoons grated lemon
Salt	zest
Freshly ground black pepper	⅓ cup heavy cream
4 chicken breasts, skinned	½ cup shredded basil leaves
and boned	Garnish:
3 tablespoons butter	Desiccated coconut
2 large garlic cloves, chopped	Raisins
2 teaspoons curry powder	Chopped apples
1 medium tomato, peeled and	
diced	

Season flour with salt and pepper on a piece of wax paper. Coat chicken with flour.

In heavy medium skillet, heat 2 tablespoons butter over medium-high heat. Add chicken and cook 8 to 10 minutes or until lightly browned and cooked through. Do not overcook. Remove to a plate.

In same skillet, melt remaining butter over medium heat. Add garlic and cook 2 minutes. Stir in curry, tomato, lemon zest, salt, and pepper and cook 3 minutes. Add cream and blend on #3 speed until combined.

Place chicken breasts in sauce and sprinkle in basil. Gently reheat 3 minutes or until heated through. Do not overcook or chicken will dry out.

Remove to warm dinner plates and sprinkle with coconut, raisins, and apples. Serves 2 to 4.

TURKEY TONNATO

4 pounds boneless turkey breast	2 tablespoons capers,
¼ teaspoon salt	undrained
¼ teaspoon freshly ground	½ cup heavy cream
black pepper	½ cup finely chopped onion
½ cup all-purpose flour	1 large garlic clove, minced
1 tablespoon butter	1 egg yolk
2 tablespoons olive oil	1 tablespoon fresh lemon juice
Sauce:	¼ teaspoon salt
6 tablespoons olive oil	¼ teaspoon freshly ground
1 can (6.5-ounce/184-g) tuna,	black pepper
drained and flaked	Garnish:
6 anchovy fillets, chopped	1 teaspoon grated lemon zest
	Lemon slices

Slice turkey breast on diagonal into cutlets. Pat turkey slices dry with paper towels; season with salt and pepper. Dredge with flour.

In large skillet, heat butter and oil; cook turkey in batches (if necessary) over medium high heat for 3 to 4 minutes on each side or until lightly browned and just cooked through. Remove turkey to platter.

Meanwhile, in beaker, place olive oil, tuna, anchovies, capers, cream, onion, garlic, egg yolk, lemon juice, salt, and pepper and blend on #6 speed until well combined.

Pour sauce over sliced turkey and chill. Garnish with lemon zest and lemon slices. Serves 4 to 6.

PORK TENDERLOIN IN RED CURRANT AND WINE SAUCE

2 pork tenderloins (each ¾ pound)	¼ teaspoon freshly ground black pepper
1 tablespoon vegetable oil	2 cups beef stock
2 tablespoons butter	1 tablespoon dry white vermouth
2 large garlic cloves, minced	
1 large shallot, chopped	¼ cup red currant jelly
¼ teaspoon salt	⅓ cup heavy cream

Trim any excess fat and membrane from tenderloins. Set aside.

In heavy skillet, heat oil and butter. Add tenderloins and cook for 5 minutes, turning to brown evenly. Remove to a plate. Drain excess fat; discard all but 1 teaspoon. Add garlic and shallot; cook, stirring for 1 minute. Stir in salt, pepper, and stock. Add tenderloins; cook, covered, over medium-low heat 30 to 35 minutes or until no longer pink inside. Take care not to boil meat.

Remove tenderloins to warm platter.

Remove skillet from heat. Add vermouth and red currant jelly; blend on #2 speed until combined. Pour in cream and blend again. Return to high heat. Cook for 10 to 15 minutes or until sauce is reduced to ¾ cup.

Slice tenderloins into ½-inch medallions; arrange on platter. Pour sauce over and serve. Serves 4.

ào

SPARERIBS WITH APPLE CINNAMON GLAZE

3 tablespoons vegetable oil	*2 tablespoons finely chopped*
6 medium garlic cloves,	*fresh ginger*
minced	*1 tablespoon Dijon mustard*
1 small onion, chopped	*½ teaspoon ground*
2 Granny Smith apples,	*cinnamon*
peeled, cored, and chopped	*¼ teaspoon ground cloves*
Grated zest of 1 large lemon	*¼ teaspoon freshly grated*
Grated zest of 1 large orange	*nutmeg*
1⅓ cups apple juice	*¼ teaspoon freshly ground*
¼ cup soy sauce	*black pepper*
¼ cup liquid honey	*4 pounds spareribs, cut into*
2 tablespoons fresh lemon	*serving portions (2-rib*
juice	*sections)*
2 tablespoons fresh orange	
juice	

In heavy medium saucepan, heat oil over medium heat. Add garlic, onion, apples, lemon and orange zest; cook for 5 minutes or until softened. Add apple juice, soy sauce, honey, lemon and orange juice, ginger, mustard, cinnamon, cloves, nutmeg, and pepper. Cook for 10 minutes; blend in saucepan on #6 speed until combined. Set aside. Cool to room temperature.

In shallow pan, pour sauce over ribs and marinate several hours or overnight in refrigerator, turning ribs occasionally.

Remove ribs from marinade and place them on broiler pan or roasting pan. Bake in a preheated 400°F oven for 45 minutes to 1 hour or until cooked, basting with marinade every 15 minutes to glaze. Serves 4 to 6.

This rib dish is quite different with the apple-cinnamon-ginger flavor, but a pleasant change from the usual barbecued ribs.

MARINATED BUTTERFLIED LEG OF LAMB

½ cup dry red wine	6 large garlic cloves, minced
½ cup olive oil	¼ teaspoon salt
½ cup fresh lemon juice	¼ teaspoon freshly ground
¼ cup fresh chopped rosemary	black pepper
¼ cup Dijon mustard	1 butterflied leg of lamb
¼ cup liquid honey	(about 3 pounds)

In medium saucepan, add red wine, oil, lemon juice, rosemary, mustard, honey, garlic, salt, and pepper. Cook on medium-high heat for about 5 minutes, blending on #3 speed until mixture is smooth and combined. Remove marinade from heat. Let cool.

Trim excess fat and membrane from lamb. Pound lamb to flatten and place in shallow glass or stainless steel baking dish. Pour marinade over lamb; marinate overnight in refrigerator, turning occasionally.

Remove lamb from marinade. Broil or barbecue 4 to 5 inches from heat or coals, brushing with marinade, for about 15 minutes on each side for medium-rare or until desired doneness. Slice thinly and serve. Serves 6.

Superb served with fresh chopped mint in raspberry vinegar, new potatoes, and Broccoli Purée (see page 164).

GRILLED LAMB CHOPS WITH MUSTARD HERB GARLIC BUTTER

½ cup butter, at room temperature	6 large garlic cloves, minced
	2 teaspoons fresh lemon juice
¼ cup Dijon mustard	½ teaspoon salt
1 tablespoon dried chervil	½ teaspoon coarsely ground
1 tablespoon dried basil	black pepper
1 tablespoon dried marjoram	4 lamb chops
1 tablespoon dried thyme	

In mixing bowl, place butter, mustard, chervil, basil, marjoram, thyme, garlic, lemon juice, salt, and pepper. Blend on #6 speed until well combined and smooth.

Grill lamb chops on a charcoal grill or under a preheated broiler until medium rare. Smooth herb butter on chops and serve. (The remaining herb butter can be formed into a roll, wrapped in wax paper, frozen, and sliced off as needed.) Serves 2. Makes about 1 cup herb butter.

A versatile butter that can also be smoothed on beef, chicken, salmon, tuna, or swordfish steaks while grilling or broiling. Top grilled vegetables, barbecued hamburgers, baked potatoes, or noodles with herb butter for a simple but tasty dinner.

STEAK WITH WINE SAUCE

2 tablespoons butter	1 cup dry red wine
3 tablespoons chopped fresh	2 tablespoons brandy
parsley	1 tablespoon Dijon mustard
2 tablespoons chopped shallots	1 teaspoon dried thyme
2 large garlic cloves, minced	¼ teaspoon freshly ground
1 green onion, chopped	black pepper
1 tablespoon all-purpose flour	3 tablespoons heavy cream
Grated zest of 1 lemon	1 2-pound sirloin steak or
1¾ cups beef stock	New York strip steaks

In heavy saucepan, melt butter over medium heat. Add parsley, shallots, garlic, and green onion; cook 3 minutes. Add flour; cook for 2 minutes, stirring with wooden spoon, on medium heat. Remove from heat; add zest, stock, wine, brandy, mustard, thyme, and pepper. Blend on #3 speed until combined; cook on high heat until liquid is reduced to 1 cup, about 15 minutes. Add cream and blend on #3 speed until combined. Set aside.

Broil steaks to taste. Pour any accumulated steak juices into sauce. Gently reheat sauce and serve with steak. Serves 4 to 6. Makes 1¼ cups sauce.

A slightly creamy, flavorful, and rich sauce.

HALIBUT STEAK WITH JULIENNE OF CARROT AND LEEK SAUCE

4 carrots, julienned	*¼ teaspoon freshly ground*
1 leek, cleaned and julienned	*black pepper*
1 pound halibut steak	*1 cup chicken stock*
¼ cup butter, at room	*½ cup dry white vermouth*
temperature	*1 tablespoon heavy cream*
¼ teaspoon salt	*1 cup packed spinach leaves,*
	julienned

On baking sheet, place a large piece of foil. Reserving half of the carrot and leek julienne, place remainder on foil. Place fish on top and dot with 1 tablespoon butter and salt and pepper. Wrap foil tightly and bake in a preheated 400°F oven for 20 to 25 minutes or until flesh is opaque and easily pierced with a fork. Remove fish and vegetables to a warm platter and pour liquid from fish into medium saucepan. Add stock and vermouth; cook over high heat until reduced to ¾ cup, about 15 to 20 minutes. Remove from heat; blend in 2 tablespoons butter and cream on #3 speed. Set aside.

In small skillet, cook remaining julienned vegetables in remaining butter for 5 minutes. Add spinach and heat through.

Pour sauce over fish and garnish with cooked carrots, leeks, and spinach.

Serves 2 to 4.

A splendid, colorful dish with its array of vegetables.

GRILLED SWORDFISH KEBABS WITH WASABI-HERB BUTTER

Marinade	Wasabi-Herb Butter
½ cup olive oil	½ cup butter, at room
3 tablespoons soy sauce	temperature
1½ tablespoons liquid honey	2 green onions, finely chopped
1 tablespoon rice wine	2 tablespoons chopped fresh
vinegar	parsley
1 teaspoon sesame oil	2 tablespoons chopped fresh
2 tablespoons finely chopped	coriander
fresh ginger	2 to 4 teaspoons wasabi
2 large garlic cloves, minced	powder, or to taste
1 green onion, finely chopped	1 teaspoon minced fresh
1 teaspoon chopped fresh	ginger
coriander	1 small garlic clove, minced
Pinch salt	18 cherry tomatoes
Freshly ground black pepper	18 green onion pieces,
2 swordfish steaks (1 pound	about 1½ inches
each), cut into 1¼-inch	
cubes	

In bowl, blend oil, soy sauce, honey, rice wine vinegar, sesame oil, ginger, garlic, green onion, coriander, salt, and pepper on #4 speed until combined.

Dry swordfish cubes with paper towel; arrange in one layer in large dish. Pour marinade over fish, toss to coat evenly and marinate for 1 hour.

In bowl, blend butter, green onions, parsley, coriander, wasabi, ginger, and garlic on #6 speed until well combined. Set aside.

Meanwhile, prepare charcoal for grilling.

When grill is ready, thread fish cubes alternating with cherry tomatoes and green onion pieces on 6 metal skewers. Grill, turning and basting frequently with marinade for about 12 minutes or until cooked through.

Transfer skewers to platter or plates and either serve with a dollop of wasabi-herb butter or spread butter on top of skewered swordfish. Serves 6.

Swordfish with an oriental inspired marinade and zippy herb butter. (Wrap and freeze remaining herb butter.) This also works well with mako shark, fresh tuna, or any kind of thick, meaty fish. Serve with rice or boiled new potatoes and a green vegetable or salad.

SHRIMP IN SAFFRON SAUCE

3 tablespoons butter	¼ teaspoon saffron threads
2 shallots, finely chopped	¼ teaspoon salt
1 garlic clove, minced	¼ teaspoon freshly ground
1 small tomato, seeded and	black pepper
chopped	½ cup heavy cream
2 cups chicken stock	¾ pound medium shrimp,
½ cup dry white vermouth	peeled and deveined

In heavy medium saucepan, melt 2 tablespoons butter over medium-high heat. Add shallots, garlic, and tomato; cook for 3 minutes, stirring, or until shallots are soft.

Add chicken stock, vermouth, saffron, salt, and pepper; blend on #4 speed until combined. Cook for 15 minutes or until reduced by half. Add cream; blend on #3 speed until combined. Cook for 2 minutes or until slightly thickened.

In small skillet, heat remaining butter. Stir in shrimp; cook for 3 minutes or until they turn pink. Do not overcook. Using slotted spoon, transfer shrimp to sauce, heat for 1 minute. Serves 4.

Serve over rice or pasta. For a sinfully rich special brunch, fill patty shells or brioches that have been hollowed out.

SALMON WITH SORREL SPINACH SAUCE

2 to 3 pounds fresh salmon fillets, skinned	6 ounces fresh spinach, chopped
¼ teaspoon salt	6 ounces fresh sorrel leaves, chopped
¼ teaspoon freshly ground black pepper	Pinch each salt, pepper, and grated nutmeg
¼ cup butter	½ cup heavy cream
½ cup chopped onion	

Sprinkle salmon with salt and pepper. Broil or grill fillets until fish flakes when lightly pressed with fork, about 8 to 10 minutes.

Meanwhile, in heavy saucepan, melt butter over medium heat. Add onion and cook 3 minutes or until soft. Add spinach, sorrel, salt, pepper, and nutmeg; cook for 5 minutes or until greens are completely wilted. Stir in cream; cook until heated through. Blend on #6 speed in saucepan until fairly smooth. Pour sauce onto heated dinner plates. Place fish on sauce. Serves 6 to 8.

Divine! Serve with boiled new potatoes and asparagus. Garnish with watercress sprigs and lemon wedges.

WELSH RAREBIT

½ cup beer	1 tablespoon Worcestershire
3 egg yolks	sauce
1 tablespoon butter	2 teaspoons dry mustard
1½ pounds Cheddar cheese,	¼ teaspoon cayenne
grated (about 6 cups)	6 slices hot toast, crusts
1 tablespoon Dijon mustard	removed, and cut into triangles

In beaker, blend beer and egg yolks on #6 speed until combined. Set aside. In top of double boiler, over simmering water, melt butter. Stir in cheese, Dijon mustard, Worcestershire sauce, dry mustard, and cayenne. When cheese has melted, gradually blend in beer-egg mixture; cook for 2 minutes or until thickened. Serve over toast points. Makes 3 cups cheese sauce. Serves 2 to 3.

Instead of using toast, you can pour rarebit onto English muffins, crumpets, or whole-grain bread. Or keep it warm and use as cheese fondue, dipping bread cubes into it.

QUICHE LORRAINE

Homemade or frozen pastry	2 extra-large eggs
(pâte brisée)	1 extra-large egg yolk
6 slices bacon, coarsely	1 teaspoon Dijon mustard
chopped	¼ teaspoon salt
1 cup (about 4 ounces) grated	¼ teaspoon freshly ground
Gruyère cheese	black pepper
1 medium onion, thinly sliced	Pinch freshly grated nutmeg
¾ cup heavy or light cream	

Line an 8-inch quiche pan or pie plate with pastry; crimp edges. Line pastry with parchment paper or aluminum foil; fill with dried beans, rice, or pie weights. Bake in 400°F oven for 10 minutes. Cool in pan on cake rack.

Meanwhile, in skillet, fry bacon until just crisp; drain on paper-towel-lined plate.

Sprinkle cheese, onion, and bacon over bottom of prebaked pastry shell.

In mixing bowl, blend cream, eggs, egg yolk, mustard, salt, pepper, and nutmeg on #2 speed with whisk attachment for 15 seconds. Pour mixture into pastry shell. Bake in a 375°F oven for 45 minutes or until egg mixture is set. Remove from oven. Let stand for 5 minutes. Slice into wedges and serve. Serves 4.

A classic standby for lunch. Serve with a crisp green salad and warm brioches.

CHAPTER SEVEN

VEGETABLES

PARSNIP PURÉE WITH PARSLEY AND CHIVES
SWEET POTATO AND CARROT PURÉE
BROCCOLI PURÉE
PURÉE OF PEAS AND MINT
MASHED POTATOES
CELERIAC (CELERY ROOT) AND POTATO PURÉE
POTATO AND CARROT PANCAKES
PAKORAS
ZUCCHINI AND EGGPLANT IN ZESTY TOMATO SAUCE
TOMATOES STUFFED WITH WHITE KIDNEY BEAN PURÉE
ASPARAGUS TIMBALE
GREEN BEANS IN VINAIGRETTE
FENNEL WITH LEEK AND DILL SAUCE
CAULIFLOWER GRATINÉE

PARSNIP PURÉE WITH PARSLEY AND CHIVES

2 pounds parsnips, peeled and cut into 2-inch pieces	2 cups (about 8 ounces) grated Havarti cheese
1 medium onion, unpeeled	2 tablespoons chopped fresh
½ teaspoon salt	chives
¼ teaspoon white pepper	2 tablespoons chopped fresh
¼ cup butter, at room temperature	parsley

In large saucepan, bring salted water to a boil. Add parsnips and onion; cover and reduce heat to medium-low. Simmer parsnips for about 45 minutes or until tender. Drain in colander. Remove and discard skin from onion.

In mixing bowl, blend parsnips, onion, salt, pepper, and butter on #6 speed until puréed. Spoon into lightly buttered gratin dish or 9 x 5-inch loaf pan. Sprinkle cheese, chives, and parsley on top. Bake at 350°F for 30 to 40 minutes or until bubbly and cheese is light golden brown. Serves 6.

Even those who don't like parsnips will love this dish. The parsnips taste buttery sweet with lots of cheese flavor. I like to serve this with a pork roast or as a holiday side dish with turkey.

SWEET POTATO AND CARROT PURÉE

2 pounds sweet potatoes	½ teaspoon freshly ground
1 pound carrots, peeled and	black pepper
cut into ¼-inch slices	⅛ teaspoon cayenne
2 cups water	½ cup sour cream
¼ cup butter	1 large sweet red pepper,
2 tablespoons sugar	seeded and finely chopped
½ teaspoon salt	

Bake sweet potatoes in 400°F oven for 1 hour or until tender when pierced with a knife. Cool and peel. Set aside.

In heavy saucepan, combine carrots, water, 2 tablespoons butter, sugar, salt, pepper, and cayenne; cook, uncovered, on high heat for about 35 minutes or until all liquid has evaporated. Add sweet potatoes to carrot mixture along with remaining butter and sour cream. Blend on #6 speed for 4 to 5 minutes or until mixture is puréed. Stir in red pepper. Serve immediately or reheat in 350°F oven, covered, for 20 minutes. Makes about 5 cups.

Superb with an Easter ham and tender, minted green peas.

BROCCOLI PURÉE

2 bunches broccoli (each 1½ pounds), florets and stems coarsely chopped	½ teaspoon salt
	½ teaspoon freshly ground black pepper
¼ cup light sour cream	¼ teaspoon freshly grated nutmeg
2 tablespoons butter	

In large saucepan, in boiling water, cook broccoli, uncovered, for 5 minutes or until tender and still bright green. Drain broccoli; return to saucepan. Add sour cream, butter, salt, pepper, and nutmeg. Blend on #6 speed until puréed. Stir mixture over low heat for 1 minute or until heated through. Serve in pretty bowl. Serves 6.

True fresh broccoli taste — serve this with Marinated Butterflied Leg of Lamb (see page 150) and new potatoes. Great for babies, too!

PURÉE OF PEAS AND MINT

4 cups (4 pounds in pod)	¼ teaspoon sugar
shelled fresh or frozen peas	¼ teaspoon salt
¼ cup butter	¼ teaspoon freshly ground
¼ cup light cream	black pepper
1 tablespoon chopped fresh mint	

In steamer, steam fresh peas for 4 minutes or until almost cooked. If using frozen, steam 2 minutes or until just heated through. Remove from steamer.

In mixing bowl, blend cooked peas with butter, cream, mint, sugar, salt, and pepper on #6 speed until puréed. Serve immediately. Makes 2 cups.

Fresh-tasting pea purée. I sometimes like to pipe or spoon it into sautéed artichoke bottoms and serve as a side dish.

MASHED POTATOES

1 pound potatoes (about 3 medium), peeled	3 tablespoons sour cream
	Salt
2 tablespoons butter	Freshly ground black pepper

In saucepan, place potatoes in cold water; bring to a boil, covered, and cook for about 25 to 30 minutes or until tender. Drain and place in mixing bowl. Add butter, sour cream, salt, and pepper to taste. On #3 speed, gently blend, moving the blender around, up and out of mixture to avoid overprocessing, until smooth. Makes 2 cups.

It's essential to use #3 speed, so that potatoes remain slightly fluffy. Mashed potatoes, real comfort food, round out many a dinner. Excellent served alongside stews or as a thickener for winter soups.

CELERIAC (CELERY ROOT) AND POTATO PURÉE

¼ cup butter	½ teaspoon salt
1¼ pounds potatoes (about 2 large), peeled and cubed	½ teaspoon freshly ground white pepper
¼ cup chopped onion	1 cup chicken stock
1 medium celery root, peeled and cubed	1 teaspoon sugar
	¼ cup light cream
1 tablespoon fresh lemon juice	

In large saucepan, melt butter over medium-high heat. Add potatoes, onion, celery root, lemon juice, salt, and pepper. Cook for 5 minutes. Stir in chicken stock and sugar. Simmer gently over medium-low heat, covered, for about 40 minutes or until vegetables are soft, stirring occasionally. Add cream and cook, stirring constantly, for about 3 minutes over high heat until almost dry. In saucepan, blend on #3 speed until smooth. Makes about 3¾ cups.

Mild and sweetly flavored, it is delicious with lamb. To enhance the celery flavor, serve with a dollop of butter and chopped fresh chives sprinkled on top.

POTATO AND CARROT PANCAKES

2 tablespoons butter	1 teaspoon dried thyme
1 small onion, finely chopped	¼ teaspoon salt
¾ cup finely shredded carrots	¼ teaspoon freshly
1 pound potatoes (about	ground pepper
3 medium), peeled	⅛ teaspoon freshly
3 tablespoons butter	grated nutmeg
1 tablespoon heavy cream	1 tablespoon vegetable oil

In small skillet, melt 1 tablespoon butter over medium heat. Add onion; cook for 3 minutes or until soft. Set aside.

Blanch carrots and refresh under cold water; drain. Set aside. Boil potatoes in large saucepan in lightly salted water for 30 to 35 minutes or until tender; drain. Return potatoes to saucepan and add 3 tablespoons butter, cream, thyme, salt, pepper, and nutmeg. Blend on #3 speed to mash potatoes, being careful not to overblend. Blend in carrots and onions on #4 speed. Form into 8 pancakes.

In heavy non-stick skillet, heat remaining 1 tablespoon butter and oil on medium heat. Fry pancakes for 7 minutes or until crisp and golden brown on both sides. Serve immediately or keep warm on baking sheet in 300°F oven. Makes 8 pancakes.

Green Chili Butter (page 32)
with corn on the cob

PAKORAS

1 cup all-purpose flour	½ teaspoon salt
1 cup water	½ teaspoon chili powder
1 jalapeño pepper, seeded	1 cup cauliflower, blanched
and finely chopped	and finely chopped
1 garlic clove, minced	¾ cup mashed potatoes
3 tablespoons chopped fresh	(see page 166)
coriander	1 medium onion, finely
2 teaspoons chopped fresh	chopped
mint or ½ teaspoon dried	3 cups vegetable oil for
1 teaspoon ground cumin	deep-frying

In mixing bowl, blend flour, water, jalapeño pepper, garlic, coriander, mint, cumin, salt, and chili powder on #6 speed until combined. Mixture will be thick. Let stand 30 minutes. Stir in cauliflower, mashed potatoes, and onion.

In deep fryer or wok, heat oil to 375°F. Drop a heaping teaspoon of potato mixture into oil. Fry 6 at a time, being careful not to overcrowd pan. Fry until golden brown, about 3 to 5 minutes, then remove with a slotted spoon to paper-towel-lined plate. Repeat with remaining mixture. Serve immediately. Makes about 22 pakoras.

Vegetable pakoras are fritters — almost like Indian tempura.

*Cream of Green Pea Soup (page 128)
and Peach Yogurt Soup (page 129)*

ﾞ☙

ZUCCHINI AND EGGPLANT IN ZESTY TOMATO SAUCE

2 tablespoons salt	1 tablespoon chopped fresh
1 eggplant (about 1 pound),	chives
unpeeled, cut into ½-inch	½ teaspoon freshly ground
slices	black pepper
4 zucchini (about 1¾	10 Greek black olives
pounds), sliced diagonally	(Kalamata), pitted and
about ½-inch thick	chopped
2 tablespoons butter	1 tablespoon capers, drained
5 large ripe tomatoes (about	¼ cup olive oil
2¼ pounds), chopped	1 large onion, thinly sliced
6 green onions, chopped	3 cups (about 12 ounces)
1 garlic clove, minced	grated mozzarella
¼ cup chopped fresh parsley	⅓ cup freshly grated
2 tablespoons chopped fresh	Parmesan cheese
basil	

Using two colanders or bowls — one for the eggplant and one for the zucchini slices — sprinkle 1 tablespoon salt over contents of each; toss to coat evenly and set aside for 30 minutes to drain. Rinse under cold running water. Dry well with paper toweling.

In heavy medium saucepan, add butter, tomatoes, green onions, garlic, parsley, basil, chives, and pepper. Cook on medium-high heat for 10 minutes or until tomatoes are soft. Blend on #4 speed until combined but still chunky. Stir in olives and capers. Set aside.

In heavy skillet, heat 1 tablespoon oil (adding more oil if necessary) and cook eggplant for 5 minutes or until soft and golden. Remove to plate.

In same skillet, add 1 tablespoon oil and cook zucchini for 2 minutes or until golden. Remove to plate.

In large baking dish, arrange one third of eggplant, zucchini, raw onion, and tomato sauce in layers. Repeat twice more. Sprinkle mozzarella and Parmesan cheese on top. Bake in a 350°F oven for 30 minutes or until cheese is bubbly and top is golden brown. Cover with foil if browning too quickly. Serves 4 to 6.

A hearty vegetarian meal or side dish that will fill your kitchen with wonderful aromas while it is cooking. No-salt is needed on account of the olives, cheese, and presalting of vegetables.

TOMATOES STUFFED WITH WHITE KIDNEY BEAN PURÉE

4 ripe tomatoes (about 2 pounds)	1 medium garlic clove, minced
	Finely grated zest of 1 lemon
1 can (19-ounce/540-mL) white kidney beans, drained and rinsed	2 tablespoons fresh lemon juice
	2 teaspoons Dijon mustard
	Salt
½ cup finely chopped fresh parsley	Freshly ground black pepper
	Garnish:
¼ cup olive oil	Finely chopped fresh parsley
2 green onions, finely chopped	Paprika

Core and scoop out tomato flesh, leaving a sturdy ¼-inch shell. Drain tomatoes, cut side down, on paper towel. Set aside.

In mixing bowl, place beans, parsley, oil, green onions, garlic, lemon zest, lemon juice, mustard, salt, and pepper to taste; blend on #6 speed until just combined. Do not overblend — it should still have some texture. Fill hollowed tomatoes with purée. Garnish with parsley and paprika. Serves 4 as a side dish or appetizer.

A refreshing, cool dish for a hot summer evening.

ASPARAGUS TIMBALE

1 bunch asparagus (about	⅓ cup (about 1½ ounces)
1 pound), trimmed and	grated Monterey Jack cheese
cut into ½ inch pieces	3 tablespoons coarsely chopped
2 tablespoons butter	fresh dill
2 leeks, cleaned and chopped	1 tablespoon Dijon mustard
(white part only)	¼ teaspoon salt
3 large eggs	¼ teaspoon freshly ground
⅔ cup heavy or light cream	black pepper

Preheat oven to 350°F.

In boiling water, blanch asparagus for 30 seconds. Drain and refresh under cold running water. Drain again; set aside.

In heavy skillet, melt butter over medium-high heat. Add leeks; cook for 10 minutes or until soft.

In mixing bowl, blend eggs, cream, cheese, dill, mustard, salt, and pepper on #4 speed until combined. Stir in asparagus and leeks.

Pour mixture into 6 well-greased 4-ounce ramekins. Place ramekins in large pan. Add enough hot water to come halfway up sides of ramekins. Bake 45 minutes or until set. Remove ramekins from pan and let rest 10 minutes on rack.

If serving hot, run knife around inside edge and turn asparagus timbales onto warmed plates. Serve with Orange Hollandaise (see page 98).

If serving cold, chill, covered, in ramekins for several hours. Serves 6.

GREEN BEANS IN VINAIGRETTE

1 pound green beans, trimmed	1 teaspoon sugar
1 egg	½ teaspoon dry mustard
1 large garlic clove, minced	½ teaspoon salt
⅓ cup vegetable oil	½ teaspoon freshly ground
1 tablespoon fresh lemon juice	black pepper

Steam green beans for 5 minutes or until tender-crisp; refresh under cold running water to stop cooking.

In beaker, place egg, garlic, oil, lemon juice, sugar, mustard, salt, and pepper. Blend on #6 speed until thickened. Pour over beans. Serve immediately or marinate for several hours in refrigerator before serving. Serves 6. Makes about ⅔ cup dressing.

This dressing is also delicious over fresh sliced tomatoes or cucumbers.

FENNEL WITH LEEK AND DILL SAUCE

¼ cup butter	¼ teaspoon freshly ground
3 leeks, cleaned and finely	black pepper
chopped (white part only)	2 bulbs fennel (about
2 large garlic cloves, minced	1¼ pounds), quartered
1 cup heavy or light cream	½ cup freshly grated
1 cup fresh dill, finely	Parmesan cheese
chopped	1 sweet red pepper, roasted
¼ teaspoon salt	and julienned

In heavy medium saucepan, melt butter over medium-low heat. Add leeks and garlic; cover, and cook for 15 minutes or until soft, stirring occasionally. Add cream, dill, salt, and pepper; blend on #4 speed until combined and thickened.

In small saucepan, in salted boiling water, cook fennel, uncovered, for about 5 minutes or until barely tender. Drain and pat dry with paper toweling. Place fennel in single layer in buttered baking dish. Pour leek mixture on top and sprinkle with Parmesan cheese. Top with red pepper. Bake uncovered in 350°F oven for 30 minutes or until bubbling and heated through. Serves 4.

Creamy and rich with wonderful flavors of dill and fennel. A good accompaniment to any fish dish, whether baked, grilled, or steamed.

177

CAULIFLOWER GRATINÉE

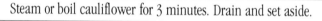

1 head cauliflower, cut into florets	½ teaspoon dried thyme
	½ teaspoon dried sage
3 tablespoons olive oil	¼ teaspoon salt
8 ounces goat cheese, at room temperature	¼ teaspoon freshly ground black pepper
½ cup plain yogurt	Pinch red pepper flakes
1 large garlic clove, minced	

Steam or boil cauliflower for 3 minutes. Drain and set aside.

In mixing bowl, blend oil, cheese, yogurt, garlic, thyme, sage, salt, pepper, and red pepper flakes on speed #6 until combined.

Place steamed cauliflower in lightly greased baking dish. Pour sauce over.

Bake at 350°F for 30 minutes or until bubbly. Serves 6.

Wonderful and garlicky — enhanced with the flavor of goat cheese.

CHAPTER EIGHT

DESSERTS

STRAWBERRY CHEESECAKE
EASY CHOCOLATE CAKE
CHOCOLATE FROSTING
FLUFFY WHITE FROSTING
APPLE FLAN
GRASSHOPPER PIE
FROZEN ORANGE CREAM PIE
LEMON CURD TARTLETS
LEMON-LIME MOUSSE
STRAWBERRY FOOL
CHOCOLATE MOUSSE
MERINGUES
PINK GRAPEFRUIT SORBET
SYLLABUB
CRÈME BRÛLÉE

STRAWBERRY CHEESECAKE

Crumb crust:	1 tablespoon cornstarch
1⅓ cups graham	1 teaspoon vanilla
cracker crumbs	Grated zest of 1 large lemon
¼ cup sugar	½ cup sugar
⅓ cup butter, melted	3 extra-large eggs, at room
Filling:	temperature
2 packages (each 8-ounce/	Glaze:
250-g) cream cheese,	½ cup apricot jam
at room temperature	1 tablespoon water
3 tablespoons butter, at room	1 tablespoon sugar
temperature	1 quart fresh strawberries,
¾ cup sour cream, at room	hulled
temperature	

In medium bowl, mix graham cracker crumbs, sugar, and butter with wooden spoon until combined. Press into bottom and sides of well buttered 9-inch round springform pan. Bake crust in preheated 375°F oven for 8 minutes. Cool completely in pan, on cake rack.

Reduce oven heat to 350°F.

In large bowl, blend cream cheese, butter, sour cream, cornstarch, vanilla, lemon zest, sugar, and eggs on #6 speed — moving blender up and around bowl until completely combined. Pour into prepared crust. Bake 1 hour or until center of cake is just barely firm to the touch. Remove from oven and immediately loosen cake from rim of pan. Place on rack; cool to room temperature and cover with plastic wrap. Chill for several hours.

Remove from refrigerator; release lock on side ring and remove cake. Leave cake on base for easier cutting.

In small heavy saucepan, heat apricot jam, water, and sugar over medium-low heat. Blend on #5 speed until jam is smooth.

Spoon a thin layer of glaze over top of cheesecake. Arrange strawberries close together with pointed ends facing upwards. Brush warm glaze (if too thick, thin out with a little more hot water) over strawberries to cover completely. Chill for several hours before serving. Serves 8.

A tempting-looking, rich, dense, and scrumptious cheesecake!

EASY CHOCOLATE CAKE

1½ cups all-purpose flour	1 cup lukewarm water
1 cup sugar	⅓ cup butter, melted
3 tablespoons unsweetened	1 extra-large egg
cocoa	1 teaspoon cider vinegar
1½ teaspoons salt	1 teaspoon vanilla
1 teaspoon baking soda	Butter

In large mixing bowl, stir together flour, sugar, cocoa, salt, and soda. Add water, butter, egg, vinegar, and vanilla; blend on #6 speed until well combined. Pour batter into buttered 8-inch square baking pan or 9-inch round cake pan. Bake in 350°F oven for 30 minutes, or until skewer inserted into center of cake comes out clean. Remove from oven; run knife around outside of cake. Cool in pan 10 minutes. Invert cake and carefully turn out onto cake rack. Cool completely. Frost with Chocolate Frosting (opposite). Cut into wedges. Makes 6 to 8 servings.

Quite a light cake. Instead of chocolate frosting, try dusting it with sifted icing sugar. Make a neat design using strips of wax paper. Lay the strips on top of the cake in a lattice design or simply in parallel lines and dust heavily with icing sugar. Or use a paper doily as a stencil. Without the icing, this cake is easily transportable to picnics or in school lunches.

CHOCOLATE FROSTING

1 cup (8 ounces) cream cheese, at room temperature	1 teaspoon vanilla
	⅛ teaspoon salt
1 cup semi-sweet chocolate chips	½ cup butter, at room temperature
3 tablespoons Triple Sec	2 cups icing sugar, sifted

In top of double boiler, over barely simmering water, place cream cheese, chocolate chips, Triple Sec, vanilla, and salt. Blend on #4 speed until chips are melted and mixture is smooth.

Remove double boiler from heat; gradually blend in butter and icing sugar on #4 speed. Makes about 2¾ cups.

A delicious, rich, creamy frosting — not overly sweet. Drizzle about 1/2 cup over Easy Chocolate Cake (opposite), or over cupcakes, vanilla cake, pound cake, or madeleines.

FLUFFY WHITE FROSTING

3 egg whites	*¼ teaspoon salt*
¾ cup sugar	*¼ teaspoon cream of tartar*
⅓ cup corn syrup	*1 teaspoon vanilla*
3 tablespoons cold water	

In top of double boiler, over boiling water, combine egg whites, sugar, corn syrup, water, salt, and cream of tartar. Blend on #6 speed for 5 minutes or until mixture has thickened. Remove from heat and blend in vanilla. Continue blending for 5 minutes or until mixture has become very thickened. Makes about 1⅓ cups.

Gooey and delicious! A pure white frosting for angel food cake or cup cakes. You can substitute maple syrup or honey for corn syrup and any number of flavorings can be substituted for vanilla, e.g. orange, lemon, almond, or peppermint.

APPLE FLAN

1 package (16-ounce/454-g)	1 egg yolk
frozen puff pastry, thawed	2 pounds Granny Smith
½ cup butter	apples (about 6), cored,
¾ cup sugar	peeled, and sliced
2 tablespoons all-purpose flour	1 tablespoon sugar
Pinch salt	¼ teaspoon ground cinnamon
2 eggs	

Lightly grease a 10-inch round flan pan with removeable bottom. Roll puff pastry to ¼-inch thickness. Line flan pan with pastry, crimping edges.

In heavy saucepan, over medium heat, stir butter and sugar together until sugar is dissolved. Stir in flour and salt and remove from heat.

In beaker, blend eggs and yolk together on #6 speed for 1 minute or until bright yellow. Blend in butter-sugar mixture on #5 speed for 2 minutes or until smooth.

Place apple slices in concentric circles on pastry. Pour sugar mixture over apples; sprinkle with sugar and cinnamon. Bake in preheated 400°F oven for 40 minutes or until crust is golden brown and apples are tender. Serves 6 to 8.

If you want to really gild the lily, serve this with crème Chantilly: in beaker, using whisk attachment, whip 1 cup heavy cream with 1 teaspoon sugar, and 1 teaspoon vanilla on #4 speed until only slightly thickened.

GRASSHOPPER PIE

4 eggs, separated	1 cup heavy cream
2/3 cup sugar	2 9-inch prepared chocolate
1 tablespoon gelatin	cookie, or graham cracker
1/2 cup cold water	crust pie shells
1/4 cup green crème de menthe	

In medium bowl, blend egg yolks and sugar together on #6 speed until well combined. Set aside.

Sprinkle gelatin over cold water in bowl. Let soak 5 minutes.

In top of double boiler, over simmering water, dissolve soaked gelatin and blend on #3 speed until clear and gelatin is dissolved. Remove top of double boiler and set aside to cool to room temperature.

Add cooled gelatin and crème de menthe to egg yolk mixture. Blend on #3 speed until combined. Set aside.

In another bowl, using whisk attachment, whisk egg whites on #2 speed until soft peaks form. Fold into egg yolk mixture.

In bowl, using whisk attachment, whip cream on #1 speed until just thickened, but not stiff. Fold into yolk mixture; pour into prepared pie shells.

Chill several hours before serving. Serves 12.

An old-fashioned — '50s kitsch — pie which you can garnish with chocolate curls.

FROZEN ORANGE CREAM PIE

6 tablespoons butter	2 eggs
⅔ cup sugar	2 egg yolks
Grated zest of 2 oranges	3 prepared 9-inch pie shells,
Grated zest of 2 lemons	baked and cooled
½ cup fresh orange juice	1½ cups heavy cream
¼ cup fresh lemon juice	1 teaspoon vanilla
Pinch salt	

In double boiler, over simmering water, melt butter with sugar, orange and lemon zest, orange and lemon juice, and salt. Blend on #5 speed until butter is melted and sugar dissolved. Remove top of double boiler and place over bowl of ice water to cool.

Meanwhile, in mixing bowl, blend eggs and yolks on #6 speed until combined. When orange-lemon mixture is cooled, blend egg mixture into orange mixture on #4 speed until combined. Set aside.

In another mixing bowl, using whisk attachment, whip cream until slightly thickened on #2 speed. Add vanilla to cream and blend just to combine. Pour cream mixture into orange-lemon mixture and blend on #4 speed until combined.

Pour into 3 pie shells and freeze, covered, for several hours or until firm. To serve, let pie sit at room temperature for 5 minutes or until easily sliced. Serves 14 to 18.

LEMON CURD TARTLETS

1 dozen prepared mini tartlet shells, fresh or frozen	Juice of 3 lemons (about ½ cup)
1 cup butter	4 egg yolks
Finely grated zest of 3 lemons	1 egg
	1½ cups sugar

Bake tartlet shells in preheated 375°F oven for about 2 minutes or until golden. Cool on cake rack.

Meanwhile in top of double boiler, over simmering water, melt butter with lemon zest and juice.

In mixing bowl, blend egg yolks and egg on #6 speed for 1 minute or until foamy. Gradually add sugar while continuing to blend, until thick and fluffy.

Quickly pour ¼ cup melted butter mixture into egg mixture; blend on #6 speed until combined. Return mixture to double boiler. Stir using wooden spoon for 5 minutes or until thickened. Cool completely. Spoon lemon curd into tartlet shells. Makes about 2¾ cups lemon curd. Makes 1 dozen mini tartlets.

Any remaining lemon curd can be poured into sterilized jars and topped with sterilized lids. Keeps in refrigerator for up to 3 months. Lemon curd is lovely spread on toast or muffins. It makes a great filling for Danish pastries and is also superb sandwiched between vanilla cake layers or even hazelnut cake layers.

LEMON-LIME MOUSSE

2 packages gelatin	1 cup lemon-lime juice (2 large
⅓ cup cold water	lemons, 2 to 4 limes)
7 extra-large eggs, separated	Garnish:
1½ cups heavy cream	1 pint strawberries, sliced
1 cup sugar	Lime slices
Finely grated zest of 4 lemons	Finely grated lime zest
Finely grated zest of 2 limes	(optional)

In small bowl, sprinkle gelatin over cold water. Set aside to soak.

In bowl, beat egg whites using whisk attachment on #2 speed until light and fluffy. Set aside.

In beaker, whisk cream on #3 speed until thickened. Set aside.

In top of double boiler, over barely simmering water, place egg yolks, sugar, lemon and lime zest, and lemon-lime juice. Blend on #3 speed until mixture is combined and thickened. Add gelatin and blend until dissolved.

Pour mixture into stainless steel or glass bowl; place bowl in ice water. Allow to stand until it just begins to set; blend on #6 speed until fluffy. Fold in egg whites and whipped cream. Pour into glass bowl and refrigerate for several hours or until chilled. Garnish with strawberries, lime slices, and lime zest if desired. Serves 6 to 8.

This is a gorgeous summer dessert. Very light with a beautiful citrus flavor.

STRAWBERRY FOOL

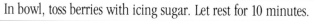

1 pint strawberries, hulled	Garnish:
and quartered	Fresh mint leaves
½ cup icing sugar	6 whole strawberries
1½ cups heavy cream	

In bowl, toss berries with icing sugar. Let rest for 10 minutes.

Meanwhile, in beaker, using whisk attachment, whisk cream on #3 speed for 3 minutes or until thickened.

Blend berries on #5 speed until puréed. Fold whipped cream into berries. Chill for at least 4 hours before serving. Garnish with strawberry halves and mint leaves. Serves 4.

Easy, light, and refreshing. Serve a light, delicate, lacy cookie with the fool — brandy snaps, almond tuiles, or the like. Very pretty served in antique wine goblets or parfait glasses topped with whipped cream or strawberries.

CHOCOLATE MOUSSE

2 cups (12 ounces) semi-sweet chocolate chips	1½ cups heavy cream
	1 teaspoon vanilla
2 tablespoons Grand Marnier	6 eggs, separated
Pinch salt	

In top of double boiler, over simmering water, combine chocolate chips, Grand Marnier, salt, and ¾ cup cream. As chips begin to melt, blend on #5 speed until combined. Stir in vanilla; remove from heat and cool to room temperature. Add egg yolks and blend on #3 speed until combined. Set aside.

In beaker, using whisk attachment, beat egg whites on #2 speed until just stiff. Fold into chocolate mixture.

In beaker, using whisk attachment, beat remaining cream on #1 speed until thickened. Fold into chocolate mixture. Pour into glass bowl and chill for several hours before serving. Serves 6 to 8.

A luscious yet simple-to-prepare dessert for chocolate fanciers. Lovely with fresh whole strawberries or whipped cream.

MERINGUES

4 extra-large egg whites	¾ teaspoon vanilla
1 cup sugar	½ teaspoon white vinegar
⅛ teaspoon salt	

In large bowl, using whisk attachment, beat egg whites on #2 speed until soft peaks form. Gradually add sugar and salt; continue whisking until stiff glossy peaks form. Whisk in vanilla and vinegar.

Onto wax-paper or parchment-paper-lined baking sheet, spoon six puffy rounds of meringue mixture. Bake in 250°F oven for about 2 hours, or until meringues are slightly colored. Turn oven off and leave meringues in oven overnight or let them cool for 8 hours. Makes 6 meringues.

Top meringues with fresh strawberries, kiwi fruit, Raspberry Sauce (see page 86), and whipped cream. Meringues can be made ahead and stored in airtight container for up to 1 week.

PINK GRAPEFRUIT SORBET

½ cup sugar	*2 cups pink grapefruit juice*
½ cup water	*(about 2 grapefruits)*
Finely grated zest of 1 pink	*1 cup orange juice (about*
grapefruit	*3 oranges)*
Finely grated zest of 3 oranges	Garnish:
	Fresh mint sprigs

In heavy saucepan, heat sugar and water over medium-high heat for 5 minutes or until dissolved. Brush sides of saucepan down with water occasionally to prevent crystals from forming. Set aside to cool to room temperature.

In saucepan, add grapefruit and orange zests and grapefruit and orange juice to sugar syrup. Blend on #3 speed until well combined.

Pour into chilled canister of ice-cream maker and freeze according to manufacturer's instructions or pour into a stainless steel bowl, cover, and freeze until ice crystals begin to form. Remove from freezer and blend on #6 speed to break up sorbet. Place back in freezer, covered, until firm. Thaw a few minutes before serving. Makes 1½ quarts.

Garnish with mint sprigs. Serve scoops inside brandy snaps or cookie tulips for a touch of elegance.

SYLLABUB

¼ cup fresh lemon juice	½ teaspoon ground cinnamon
⅓ cup tawny port	¼ teaspoon almond extract
⅓ cup superfine sugar	1½ cups heavy cream
Finely grated zest of 2 lemons	8 macaroon cookies

In mixing bowl, blend lemon juice, port, sugar, zest, cinnamon, and almond extract on #4 speed for 2 minutes or until sugar dissolves and mixture is foamy.

Crumble macaroons into bottom of pretty glass bowl or 8 individual dessert dishes. Pour mixture over crumbled cookies.

In bowl, whip cream using whisk attachment on #1 speed until soft peaks form. Spread over mixture and chill for several hours before serving. Serves 6.

Another way of preparing this dessert is to incorporate the port-macaroon mixture into the whipped cream. The color changes to light ruby, so it may not appear as attractive, but the taste is fabulous.

CRÈME BRÛLÉE

2 cups heavy cream	Pinch salt
2 tablespoons sugar	4 extra-large egg yolks
1 teaspoon vanilla	¾ cup light brown sugar

In medium saucepan, over medium heat, blend cream, sugar, vanilla, and salt on #2 speed; bring to a simmer. Set aside.

In mixing bowl, beat egg yolks on #6 speed for 1 minute. Pour hot cream mixture into yolks; blend on #3 speed, just until incorporated. Do not overbeat.

Divide mixture evenly into 6 4-ounce ramekins and place in shallow baking pan. Pour hot water in pan to reach halfway up ramekins. Bake 2 hours in 250°F oven, or until knife comes out clean when inserted in center of custard. Remove ramekins from pan; refrigerate for several hours.

Sift brown sugar onto each custard, making sure it is smooth. Set custards under preheated broiler. Broil for about 1 minute, or until sugar begins to caramelize. Remove ramekins immediately; chill before serving. Serves 6.

Creamy, rich, and absolutely delicious! Dark brown-sugar coating on top of custards hardens and is delicious with a spoonful of creamy custard. When caramelizing sugar, take care that it doesn't burn.

CHAPTER NINE

DRINKS

TOFU BANANA SHAKE
PIÑA COLADA SHAKE
PAPAYA SHAKE
VANILLA MILKSHAKE
STRAWBERRY ORANGE JUICE
ORANGE BANANA DRINK
ORANGE HONEY DRINK
MARGARITA
LOW-CAL STRAWBERRY CANTALOUPE DRINK
PEACH BUTTERMILK LOW-CAL DRINK
EGGNOG
HOT CHOCOLATE WITH MARSHMALLOWS
CHOCOLATE BANANA LOW-CAL DRINK
FROTHY LEMON GIN DRINK
CHOCOLATE MALTED MILK
PEACH FIZZ
FROZEN ORANGE STRAWBERRY DRINK

TOFU BANANA SHAKE

4 ounces tofu, drained	Pinch nutmeg
1 ripe banana	Crushed ice
1 cup plain yogurt	Garnish:
1 tablespoon liquid honey	Fresh strawberries
1 teaspoon vanilla	

In beaker, blend tofu, banana, yogurt, honey, vanilla, and nutmeg on #6 speed until smooth. Add ice. Garnish with strawberries. Serves 2.

The banana flavor shines through. Creamy thick — you could eat this with a spoon. Try variations on this shake by using fresh berries, pineapple, or mango. Tofu adds nutrition and texture. It is also great as a topping for granola in the morning.

Note: Do not use your hand blender to crush ice. It will damage the blade.

PIÑA COLADA SHAKE

½ cup sweetened cream of coconut	¾ cup pineapple juice
	½ cup vanilla ice cream
1 can (14-ounce/398-mL) pineapple chunks, drained	Crushed ice

In bowl, blend cream of coconut, pineapple chunks, pineapple juice, and ice cream on #6 speed until thick and foamy. Divide between 2 tall glasses. Stir in crushed ice. Serves 2.

Like a quick trip to the Caribbean — refreshing, laced with the freshness of pineapple and coconut. Add rum and enjoy a gorgeous Piña Colada. Garnish with a pineapple wedge.

PAPAYA SHAKE

1 papaya, peeled, seeded, and diced	½ cup vanilla or strawberry ice cream, softened
Finely grated zest of 2 oranges	1 tablespoon liquid honey
1 cup fresh orange juice	Crushed ice

In beaker, blend papaya, orange zest, orange juice, ice cream, and honey on #6 speed until frothy. Pour over ice in glasses and serve. Serves 2.

A very thick, creamy pale orange drink, rich in Vitamin C. Makes a great brunch or pick-me-up drink.

VANILLA MILKSHAKE

1 cup milk	2 teaspoons vanilla
1 cup vanilla ice cream, softened	

In beaker, blend milk, ice cream, and vanilla on #6 speed until thick and frothy. Serves 2.

A simple, old-fashioned milkshake. Add a ripe banana for more thickness and nutrition. Or make a peanut butter and banana shake: add 1 ripe banana and 2 tablespoons peanut butter.

STRAWBERRY ORANGE JUICE

6 large strawberries	1 teaspoon fresh lemon juice
1½ cups fresh orange juice	

In beaker, blend berries, orange juice, and lemon juice on #6 speed for about 20 seconds or until smooth. Serves 2.

Enjoy this fresh, fruity drink on a hot summer evening. It's packed with vitamin C. Garnish with whole berries, if desired.

Top: Frozen Orange Strawberry Drink (page 216)
Right: Papaya Shake (page 200)
Bottom: Strawberry Orange Juice (recipe this page)
Left: Tofu Banana Shake (page 198)
Center: Peach Buttermilk Low-Cal Drink (page 209)

ORANGE BANANA DRINK

1 cup fresh orange juice	1 tablespoon liquid honey
1 ripe banana	1 cup vanilla ice cream,
1 extra-large egg	softened

In beaker, blend orange juice, banana, egg, honey, and ice cream on #6 speed until smooth and frothy. Serves 2.

Very orangey with a hint of banana flavor. Delicious.

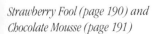

Strawberry Fool (page 190) and
Chocolate Mousse (page 191)

ORANGE HONEY DRINK

1 can (12.5-ounce/355-mL)	2 extra-large eggs
frozen, unsweetened	2 tablespoons liquid honey
orange juice concentrate	Crushed ice
4½ cups cold water	Fresh mint sprigs

In beaker, blend orange juice concentrate and water on #6 speed until combined. Add eggs and honey; blend until frothy. Pour into tall glasses. Add crushed ice. Garnish with mint sprigs if desired. Serves 6.

A light, creamy, intensely orange-flavored drink. Perfect for a mid-morning pick-me-up thirst quencher.

MARGARITA

Lime wedge	1 shot (1½ ounces) fresh lime
Salt	juice
1 shot (1½ ounces) tequila	Crushed ice
1 shot (1½ ounces) Triple Sec	

Use wedge of lime to moisten rim of 1 glass. Place salt on small plate; dip moistened rim into salt to coat. Set aside.

In beaker, blend tequila, Triple Sec, and lime juice on #5 speed until frothy. Place crushed ice in glass and pour tequila mixture over ice. Serve at once.

Serves 1.

From south of the border comes this tart and refreshing cocktail. This is my version, not too sweet, and positively thirst-quenching!

Low-cal Strawberry Cantaloupe Drink

1 cup skim milk	½ small cantaloupe, chopped
⅓ cup low-fat plain yogurt	2 teaspoons liquid honey
6 to 7 large (about 1 cup) strawberries	½ teaspoon vanilla

In beaker, blend milk, yogurt, strawberries, cantaloupe, honey, and vanilla on #6 speed for 2 minutes or until frothy. Serves 2.

A pale strawberry-colored drink — a very pleasant combination.

PEACH BUTTERMILK
LOW-CAL DRINK

1 cup buttermilk	*1 tablespoon liquid honey*
2 ripe peaches, sliced	*½ teaspoon vanilla*

In beaker, blend buttermilk, peaches, honey, and vanilla on #6 speed for 2 minutes or until frothy. Chill for 1 hour before serving, blend again. Serves 2.

An excellent, very fresh-tasting drink with a slight sour taste from the buttermilk.

EGGNOG

2 eggs	⅓ cup milk
1½ tablespoons sugar	Crushed ice
3 ounces light rum	Freshly grated nutmeg
⅔ cup heavy cream	

In beaker, blend eggs and sugar on #6 speed until combined. Add rum, cream, and milk; blend for 1 minute or until frothy. Divide crushed ice between 2 glasses; pour eggnog over ice and grate nutmeg on top. Serves 2.

A light and delicious version of everyone's favorite Christmas cocktail.

HOT CHOCOLATE WITH MARSHMALLOWS

1 tablespoon unsweetened cocoa	½ cup chocolate or vanilla ice cream, softened
1 tablespoon sugar	2 tablespoons semi-sweet chocolate chips
1 tablespoon milk	
1 cup milk	1¼ cups miniature marshmallows

In deep medium saucepan, blend cocoa, sugar, and 1 tablespoon milk until smooth. Add remaining milk and cook, stirring, over medium heat for about 5 minutes or until milk simmers. Add ice cream, chocolate chips, and 1 cup marshmallows. Stir until chocolate chips and marshmallows are melted, about 3 to 4 minutes. Remove saucepan from heat and blend on #6 speed until foamy. Pour into cups and top with remaining marshmallows. Serves 2.

Mmmmmmm . . . good and chocolatey!

CHOCOLATE BANANA LOW-CAL DRINK

1 ripe banana, sliced	*3 tablespoons instant*
1 cup skim milk	*chocolate powder*
	½ teaspoon vanilla

In beaker, blend banana, milk, chocolate powder, and vanilla on #6 speed for 2 minutes or until frothy. Serves 2.

Milk-chocolatey good! The banana gives it some thickness.

~~

FROTHY LEMON GIN DRINK

1 can (12.5-ounce/355-mL)	2 extra-large eggs
frozen pink lemonade,	Garnish:
thawed	Orange wedge, strawberries,
1½ cups water	or raspberries, and mint
¾ cup chilled gin	leaves

In 8-cup bowl, blend lemonade and water on #6 speed until combined. Add gin and eggs; blend on #6 speed until combined and frothy. Pour into punch bowl. Garnish with fresh fruit or mint or ladle over ice cubes in tall glasses and garnish with fresh fruit and mint. Serves 4.

Pleasant, light, tangy flavor. A great drink on a humid evening.

CHOCOLATE MALTED MILK

⅓ cup Horlick's malted drink powder	1 teaspoon vanilla
	1 cup milk
1 tablespoon unsweetened cocoa powder	1 cup chocolate ice cream, softened
2 tablespoons liquid honey	

In beaker, blend malted drink powder, cocoa, honey, and vanilla on #6 speed until combined. Add milk and ice cream; blend again until smooth. Serves 2.

A sweet-dreams bedtime drink!

PEACH FIZZ

1 cup dry white wine	¼ cup club soda
1 tablespoon peach schnapps	Garnish:
1 peach or nectarine,	Fresh mint sprigs
peeled and chopped	

In beaker, blend wine, peach schnapps, and peach on #6 speed until frothy and fruit is puréed. Stir in soda and pour over ice in tall glasses. Garnish with mint sprigs. Serves 2.

Refreshing, cool drink for a hot humid evening.
Try sparkling white wine for even more fizz!

FROZEN ORANGE STRAWBERRY DRINK

1 can (12.5-ounce/355 mL)	6 fresh strawberries, hulled
frozen unsweetened	1 extra-large egg
orange juice concentrate	Garnish:
1½ cups club soda	5 whole strawberries
¾ cup chilled gin	

In deep 8-cup bowl, blend orange juice concentrate, soda, gin, strawberries, and egg on #6 speed until smooth and well combined. Pour into glasses and garnish with fresh strawberries. Serves 5.

Pretty apricot color with red flecks from the straw-berries. Cool and refreshing by the pool or on the patio.

CHAPTER TEN

BABY FOODS

PURÉE OF GREEN BEANS
PURÉE OF BEETS
MEAT AND VEGETABLE PURÉE
PURÉE OF FISH
PURÉE OF PEARS
PEACH PURÉE

PURÉE OF GREEN BEANS

¾ pound green beans,
trimmed and sliced

In heavy saucepan, bring enough water to cover beans, to a boil. Add beans and simmer, uncovered, for 10 to 15 minutes or until tender. Place cooked beans in beaker and blend on #6 speed until smooth. Add a little cooking liquid, if necessary, to moisten purée. Makes about 1 cup.

PURÉE OF BEETS

2 pounds beets

Scrub beets gently. Remove tops about one inch from the beetroot.

In large heavy saucepan, place unpeeled beets in cold water to cover. Bring to a boil. Over medium heat cook beets, covered, for about 1 hour or until tender. Remove beets from liquid, reserving liquid in pan. Peel and dice beets.

In mixing bowl, blend beets on #6 speed until smooth. Add a little beet water, if necessary, to moisten purée. Makes about 3 cups.

MEAT AND VEGETABLE PURÉE

1 pound boneless beef or	*1 carrot, finely diced*
lamb, trimmed and diced	*3 cups unsalted chicken stock*
2 small potatoes, peeled and	
diced	

In heavy saucepan, combine beef or lamb, potatoes, carrot, and stock. Simmer, covered, for 50 to 60 minutes or until meat is extremely tender. Strain, reserving liquid. Set aside.

Separate meat from vegetables. In bowl, blend meat on #6 speed with ⅔ cup cooking liquid until puréed, adding more liquid if necessary. In beaker, blend vegetables on #4 speed until puréed. Makes 1½ cups meat purée; ½ cup vegetable purée.

PURÉE OF FISH

4 ounces white fish	*¼ cup 2 percent milk*
(cod or sole)	

In heavy skillet, combine fish and milk. Cook, covered, over low heat for 5 to 7 minutes or until fish flakes easily with fork. Add more milk if necessary.

In mixing bowl, blend fish mixture on #6 speed for 1 minute or until smooth. Makes about 1 cup.

PEACH PURÉE

3 ripe peaches or nectarines,   *¾ cup cold water*
peeled, pitted, and chopped

In medium saucepan, bring peaches and water to a boil. Simmer, uncovered, for 15 minutes or until almost all of liquid is absorbed and has become syrupy. Place in beaker and blend on #4 speed until smooth. Makes about 1 cup.

PURÉE OF PEARS

3 ripe pears, peeled, cored,   *1 cup cold water*
and chopped

In medium saucepan, combine pears and water. Cook, uncovered, on medium-high heat for about 20 minutes or until almost all liquid has evaporated. Place in mixing bowl, blend pear mixture on #6 speed until smooth. Makes 1½ cups.

GLOSSARY

No matter what the recipe, when it comes to selecting ingredients, buy the freshest, in-season produce as well as top-quality ingredients such as olive oils, condiments, herbs, and spices. The best ingredients will always give you superior results.

ASIAGO: An Italian cheese with a flavor milder than, but similar to provolone cheese. Freshly grated, it is lovely over pasta, pizza, or other Italian dishes as a change from Parmesan cheese.

AVOCADO: A green or purple, pear shaped fruit grown in California and Florida. If not ripe when purchased, let sit at room temperature to ripen. A little lemon juice sprinkled on pulp will prevent it from darkening.

BLACK OLIVES: I prefer black olives from Greece (Kalamata) or from France (Niçoise) because they are very pungent and flavorful. They are available from specialty food shops, many cheese shops, and some supermarket deli counters.

BLACK PEPPER: Always use freshly ground black pepper. Preground pepper has lost most of its flavor.

BOURSIN: A creamy, white French cheese flavored with garlic and herbs or coated with black pepper.

BUTTER: The recipes in this book use salted butter unless otherwise specified. Many recipes specify butter to be at room temperature so that it is softened enough to blend easily.

CAMBOZOLA: A creamy-textured, mild blue cheese from West Germany.

CAPERS: These are the pickled flower buds of a Mediterranean shrub. I prefer the Italian and Spanish varieties packed in vinegar. Never rinse them.

CHICKPEAS: A variety of legumes also called garbanzos. The canned variety is used in these recipes.

CORIANDER: A pungent green herb also called Chinese parsley or cilantro.

CREAM: Heavy or whipping cream contains at least 35% butterfat. Light cream contains 18 to 20% and is therefore lower in calories and does not whip or thicken. For those concerned with reducing calories, some recipes list both. The choice is yours.

CREAM CHEESE: For best flavor, purchase a good quality cream cheese — preferably one freshly made by a local dairy or cheesemaker. It is available in most cheese shops, supermarkets, and specialty food shops. Many recipes specify cream cheese to be at room temperature so that it is softened enough to blend easily.

CREAM OF COCONUT: Also known as coconut cream, it is used for mixing with Piña Coladas and is available canned in the soft drink/mixed drink section of supermarkets and many specialty shops.

CRUDITÉS: These are assorted raw and blanched vegetables usually served with a dip.

CURRY POWDER: It is not a single spice, but a condiment made up of some

16 to 20 spices, including ginger, turmeric, cumin, cloves, cinnamon, fenu-greek, coriander, and cayenne. You can make your own or buy a quality brand for best results.

FLAVORED BUTTERS: Also known as compound butters. Butter is combined with seasonings and herbs to enhance vegetables, soups, or as bastes to grilled and roasted meats, fish, and poultry. To store, place butter on plastic wrap or wax paper and smooth into a cylinder shape. Roll up and twist both ends to seal. Freeze and slice off pieces as needed.

GARLIC: Avoid powdered garlic. Purchase fresh garlic and choose carefully to make sure it is firm — not dried out or sprouting. Old garlic is bitter.

GOAT CHEESE: Also known as chèvre, it is a cheese made from goat's milk. These recipes use the mild, soft variety available in cheese shops and many supermarkets.

GREEN CHILIES: The canned variety are available in Mexican food shops or the Mexican food section of many supermarkets.

HEAVY CREAM: See Cream.

HERBS: It is almost always preferable to use fresh herbs. However, if using dried herbs (and spices) be sure they are of recent vintage and have not lost their color or aroma — and hence their flavor. Buy in small amounts if possible and replace them as necessary.

LEEKS: To clean, slice leek in half lengthwise, leaving root intact. Place under cold, running water, fanning the sections as necessary to remove sand. Drain well and slice.

MONTEREY JACK CHEESE: Also called simply Jack, this mild-flavored, cream-colored cheese is related to Cheddar. It has wonderful melting qualities and is often used in place of mozzarella.

NUTMEG: Always purchase whole nutmegs and grate them just before using for best flavor.

OLIVE OIL: I prefer a good-quality *virgin* or *extra-virgin* olive oil with a delicate olive taste for cooking and salad making. Try different brands because price doesn't always equate with quality.

PARMESAN CHEESE: Purchase a wedge of Parmesan cheese rather than the tasteless prepackaged variety. It is available at well-stocked cheese stores or Italian food shops. Ask to see the rind, which should read "Parmigiano Reggiano" or, second best, "Grana Padano."

REFRIED BEANS: Available canned in the Mexican food section of many supermarkets or in Mexican food shops.

SESAME SEEDS: Unless otherwise specified, recipes calling for sesame seeds require the white, untoasted form. To toast, place sesame seeds in an unoiled, heavy skillet. Place on moderate heat and cook, shaking or stirring gently, until very lightly browned. Watch carefully because they burn easily.

SUGAR: Unless otherwise specified, recipes calling for sugar require granulated sugar.

SUN-DRIED TOMATOES: Italian sun-dried tomatoes come in jars packed in olive oil. Chewy and intensely flavored, they are delicious in pasta sauces, salad dressings, and on pizzas. They are available in Italian and specialty food shops.

TOMATOES: Purchase fresh, flavorful, and unwaxed tomatoes for best results. There is no need to peel unless specified in the recipe. To peel, cut an X in non-stem end and place in boiling water for 15 seconds. Remove, refresh under cold water, and peel. To seed, cut tomatoes in half crosswise and squeeze out seeds and liquid gently.

WHITE KIDNEY BEANS: Also known as cannellini beans. I use the canned variety in these recipes. They are usually drained in a colander and gently rinsed under cold water to remove thick brine. Purchase a good brand — the beans should be whole and not mushy.

ZEST: The colored outer layer of skin on a citrus fruit. Use *only* the colored portion because the white part is bitter.

METRIC EQUIVALENTS

NOTE: *All conversions are approximate. They have been rounded off to the nearest convenient measure.*

WEIGHT:		
	¼ ounce	7 grams
	½ ounce	15 grams
	1 ounce	25 grams
	¼ pound	125 grams
	½ pound	250 grams
	¾ pound	350 grams
	1 pound 1⅔ ounces	500 grams
	2 pound 3½ ounces	1 kilogram

VOLUME:		
	¼ teaspoon	1 milliliters
	½ teaspoon	2 milliliters
	¾ teaspoon	4 milliliters
	1 teaspoon	5 milliliters
	1 tablespoon	15 milliliters
	2 tablespoons	25 milliliters
	3 tablespoons	50 milliliters
	¼ cup	50 milliliters
	⅓ cup	75 milliliters
	½ cup	125 milliliters
	⅔ cup	150 milliliters
	¾ cup	175 milliliters
	1 cup	250 milliliters

TEMPERATURES:		
	Farenheit	Celsius
	212°F	100°C
	250°F	121°C
	300°F	149°C
	350°F	177°C
	400°F	204°C
	450°F	232°C
	500°F	260°C
	550°F	288°C

INDEX

D

E

ABOUT THE AUTHOR

Joie Warner is a best-selling cookbook author. Her books include All the Best Pasta Sauces, All the Best Salads and Salad Dressings, All the Best Pizzas, The Complete Book of Chicken Wings, and she is also one of the contributors to A Basketful of Favorites. As well, Joie is a freelance food writer, a food consultant, and has appeared on several radio and TV shows. She is a professional member of both the International Association of Cooking Professionals and The American Institute of Wine & Food.